A Christmas

Storybook

For the Young and Young at Heart

Cascia Books
Enrich Your Life & Live the Faith

ISBN - 978-1-988643-03-8

Table of Contents

Introduction

A Child's Preparation for Christmas

To little boys and girls and to all good Christian people, the feast of Christmas means more than a time to give and receive gifts. To them it is a reminder of the greatest of all gifts that the world has ever received, Jesus Himself. Jesus gave Himself to us on the day He came into the world. He comes into your hearts each time you earnestly wish Him to come to you. You see that you ought to prepare your hearts well so that when Jesus comes to you on Christmas Day, He will find your hearts a beautiful place, pure and clean and ready for Him.

Just watch how carefully your dear mother cleans the house for Christmas. She wants everything to be spotless and shining. So, too, your heart ought to be pure and clean, that is, free from sin. Jesus will love to come into the hearts of those children who try to be obedient, kind, pure and simple. Now is the time for you to begin preparing your heart for Jesus. When Mary and Joseph arrived in Bethlehem, they could find no other shelter than a poor stable. I hope that when Jesus comes to you on Christmas morning, He will find your heart ready for Him and then you will not turn Him away from you.

All people who truly love God prepare their hearts for the coming of Jesus on Christmas Day. Many people do not think of Jesus and what He did for us when they make ready for Christmas. They are thinking only what pleasure they can get out of the feast, what gifts they will receive and what they will eat on that day. Jesus loved us so much that He came from His beautiful home in heaven to live and suffer and die upon earth for the love of us. He became a little child to teach us that we must always have hearts pure and innocent like those of little children.

Let us think now about what you can do to make your heart ready for the Infant Jesus. If you had been living when our Blessed Lady and St. Joseph were looking for a place of shelter on that cold winter's night and they had come to your house, would you have refused to let them in? How proud you would have been to give them your own room, your own bed! I am sure you would gladly have given your warm clothes to the Blessed Mother for the Infant Jesus. I am sure when you heard the story of the Birth of Jesus for the first time, you felt sorry that you were not living in Bethlehem for you would gladly have given Jesus a warm and comfortable shelter. You can do this even now, though Jesus is no longer a little child. How can you give Jesus shelter? By giving Him your heart as a resting place. Jesus is God. He can come into your heart if you ask Him to do so. You must earnestly wish for Jesus to come to you and He will come into your heart.

~ *Practical Aids for Catholic Teachers*

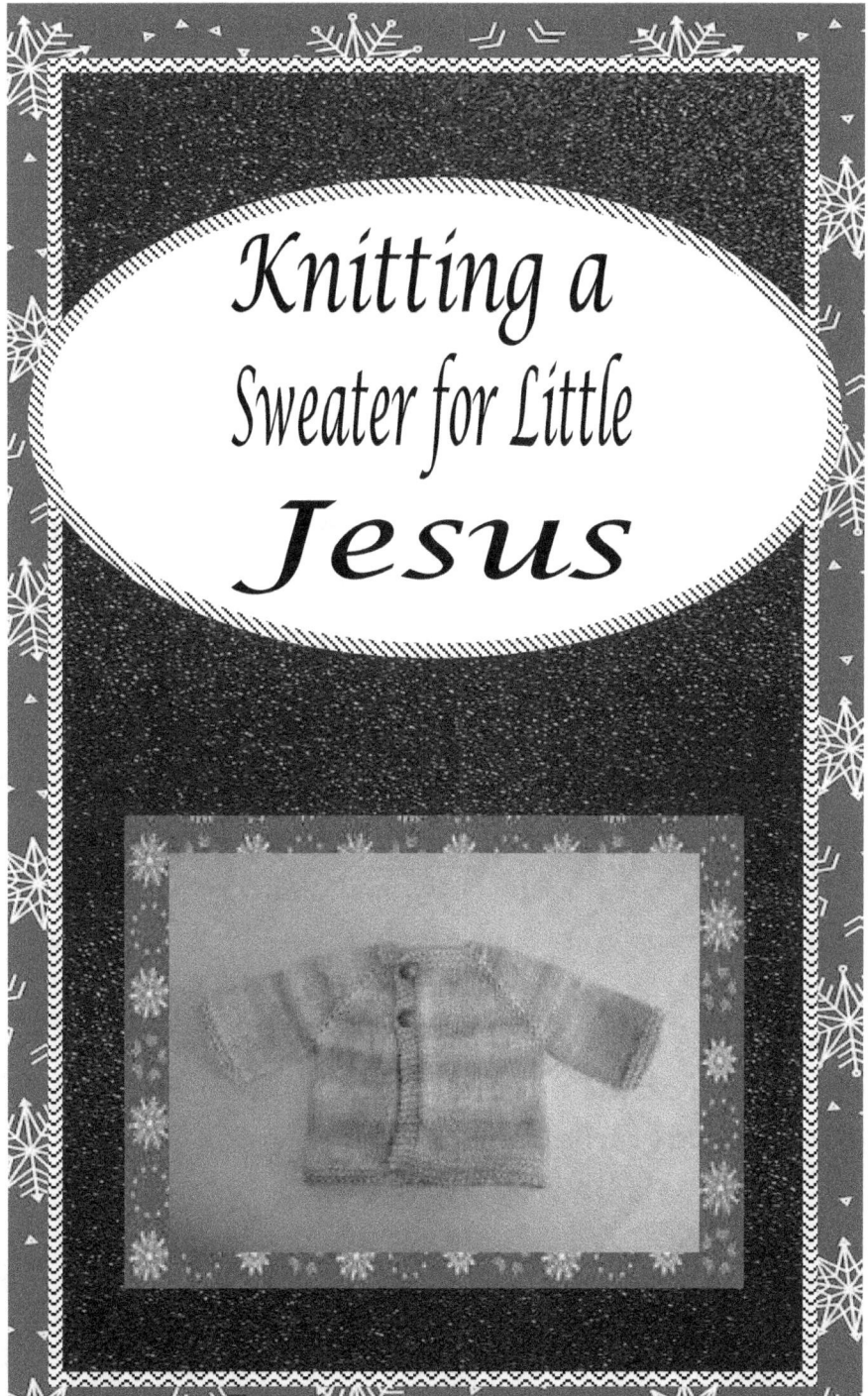

Knitting a
Sweater for Little
Jesus

It was during Advent: the four weeks of solemn preparation for the most beautiful feast of the year: Christmas. All over the world, Holy Church was longing for the coming of the Saviour, and giving expression to that longing in Her Sublime liturgy. But I am going to speak today of only two devout children of Mother Church. I know, of course, that many others were doing good during that Sacred Season of expectation, but I do not know just what form their goodness was taking. I only know about Harry and Rosie. Harry was Rosie's brother, and she wouldn't have exchanged him for anything in the world.

Advent was just beginning, and I noticed that Harry and Rosie were a little different from what they used to be. Their morning prayers were a little longer, and so were their evening prayers. They did not talk as much as they used to. Instead of shouting and laughing and playing during all their free time, they would often slip away into some quiet cozy corner. And once when I peeked into two such cozy corners, I saw Harry reading a fine book of Bible Stories, and Rosie all engrossed in a Catholic magazine. I was puzzled. So one day when I went over to the school, I told Sister about it, and asked her what these two were up to.

"Why, Father, I really do not know," she replied, "they are so mysterious about it. They are just perfect children at school now, and every day, morning, noon and night, and sometimes at recess, they make private visits to the church, and pray most devoutly before the Blessed Sacrament. Once when I entered the Church very quietly, I heard Rosie say the Our Father aloud, very piously. She thought she was all alone with Jesus. It seems to me, Father, that these two have some little plan or something."

"Leave it to me, Sister. I will find out," I said. So that very day I got a chance to be alone with Harry and Rosie. I had a little visit with them, during which they were bright and talkative, but delightfully respectful and reserved at the same time. When I arose to go, I said, "Sister and I have both noticed that you are doing something special for somebody during Advent. Tell me, what is it, darlings?"

You should have seen them blush. Finally Rosie said, "Well, Father, I'll tell you. We're knitting a sweater for little Jesus."

"Oh, I see," I replied, so surprised I didn't know what else to say. But honestly, I did not see at all. I told Sister about it. She simply said, "I wonder." Neither of us had ever seen them knitting a single stitch.

It was Christmas Eve. Harry and Rosie rang the bell at the Sisters' house, and asked to see their dear teacher. In a moment, she came, tired from the day's work of preparation for the great feast that was to begin with Midnight Mass, but happy and already full of Christmas peace and joy. Harry did the speaking. "Sister," he said, "we just finished knitting our sweater for Little Jesus. Please, Sister, put it right near the cradle of straw in the crib, so that Mother Mary can find it easily, and put it on Him to keep Him warm."

Then with a polite 'good-bye' they skipped away, leaving an envelope in Sister's hand. She opened it. Neatly written on a sheet of paper were the words,

"Dearest Christ Child, here is something that will keep Your Heart warm with love for us. 800 Our Fathers, and each word of that beautiful prayer You Yourself taught us, a well made stitch in the warm garment we want you to have on Christmas Day. Your loving,

Harry and Rosie Nearling"

It was Christmas morning. Harry and Rosie were chatting with Sister. "Oh, it was easy," Rosie was saying. "Each of us said ten Our Fathers every day: two in the morning at our morning prayers; two in the evening, at our evening prayers; and the rest during special little visits to the Blessed Sacrament."

"Sure it was easy," said Harry, "and Sister, is it possible to tell how very, very happy I am today, because I helped Rosie knit a sweater for Little Jesus."

Then everybody smiled, such a Christmas smile as you never saw before.

King John's Christmas

A. A. Milne

King John was not a good man –
He had his little ways.
And sometimes no one spoke to him
For days and days and days.
And men who came across him,
When walking in the town
Gave him a supercilious stare,
Or passed with noses in the air –
And bad King John stood dumbly there,
Blushing beneath his crown.

King John was not a good man,
And no good friends had he.
He stayed in every afternoon …
But no one came to tea.
And, round about December,
The cards upon his shelf
Which wished him lots of Christmas cheer,
And happiness in the coming year,
Were never from his near and dear,
But only from himself.

King John was not a good man,
Yet had his hopes and fears
They'd given him no presents now
For years and years and years.
But every year at Christmas,
While minstrels stood about,
Collecting tribute from the young
For all the songs they might have sung,
He stole away upstairs and hung
A hopeful stocking out.

King John was not a good man,
He lived his life aloof;
Alone he thought a message out
While climbing up the roof.
He wrote it down and propped it
Against the chimney stack;
"TO ALL AND SUNDRY – NEAR AND FAR –
F. CHRISTMAS IN PARTICULAR."
And signed it not "Johannes R."
But very humbly, "JACK."

"I want some crackers,
And I want some candy;
I think a box of chocolates
Would come in handy;
I don't mind oranges,
I do like nuts!
And I SHOULD like a pocket-knife
That really cuts.
And, oh! Father Christmas, if you love me at all,
Bring me a big, red india-rubber ball!"

King John was not a good man –
He wrote this message out,
And gat him to his room again,
Descending by the spout.
And all that night he lay there,
A prey to hopes and fears.
"I think that's him a-coming now,"
(Anxiety bedewed his brow.)
"He'll bring one present, anyhow –
The first I've had for years."

"Forget about the crackers,
And forget about the candy;
I'm sure a box of chocolates
Would never come in handy:
I don't like oranges,
I don't want nuts,
And I HAVE got a pocket-knife
That almost cuts.
But oh! Father Christmas, if you love me at all,
Bring me a big, red india-rubber ball!"

King John was not a good man –
Next morning when the sun
Rose up to tell a waiting world
That Christmas had begun,
And people seized their stockings,
And opened them with glee,
And crackers, toys and games appeared,
And lips with sticky sweets were smeared,
King John said grimly: "As I feared,
Nothing again for me!"

"I did want crackers,
And I did want candy;
I know a box of chocolates
Would come in handy;
I do love oranges,
I did want nuts.
I haven't got a pocket-knife –
Not one that cuts.
And, oh! if Father Christmas had loved me at all,
He would have brought a big, red india-rubber ball!"

King John stood by the window,
And frowned to see below
The happy bands of boys and girls
All playing in the snow.
A while he stood there watching,
And envying them all …
When through the window big and red
There hurtled by his royal head,
And bounced and fell upon the bed,
An india-rubber ball!

AND, OH, FATHER CHRISTMAS,
MY BLESSINGS ON YOU FALL
FOR BRINGING HIM
A BIG, RED,
INDIA-RUBBER
BALL!

The Legend of the
Christmas Rose

On a cold December night, everybody was coming to see their new Savior and brought Him all kinds of gifts and presents. The three Wise Men came in with their valuable gifts of myrrh, frankincense and gold and offered them to Baby Jesus.

At that point, a shepherdess, Madelon, who had seen the wise men passing through, reached the door of the stable, to see the Child. However, being very poor and having brought nothing to offer to the Child, she felt helpless and started weeping quietly at the sight of all the wonderful gifts that the Three Wise Men had got for the Child. Earlier, she had searched, in vain, for flowers all over the countryside but there was not even a single bloom to be found in the bitter winter.

An angel outside the door was watching over her and knew about her fruitless search. He took pity on her and, when he saw her head drooped down in sorrow, decided to help her with a little miracle. He gently brushed aside the snow at her feet and where her tears had fallen, sprang a beautiful cluster of waxen white winter roses with pink tipped petals. Then he softly whispered into the shepherdess' ear that these Christmas roses are far more valuable than any myrrh, frankincense or gold, for they are pure and made of love.

The maiden was pleasantly surprised when she heard those words and joyfully gathered the flowers and offered them to the Holy Infant, who, seeing that the gift was reared with tears of love, smiled at her with gratitude and satisfaction. Thus, the Christmas rose came to symbolize hope, love and all that is wonderful in this season.

The Wall of Snow

At the time when the armies of Napoleon I overran Europe, the inhabitants of a lonely and secluded farmhouse, situated very near the town of Schleswig, were greatly alarmed on hearing that the enemy was approaching that town. They had seen the sky coloured crimson by the reflection of numerous conflagrations on the path of the hostile troops, and they feared lest before entering the town the soldiers would make a raid on their farm, lay hands on all they could find, drive out the inmates and set fire to the house, as they had done in many other instances.

All night through, while listening for the tramp of the dreaded invaders, the family prayed earnestly to God for His protection. The old grandmother was most assiduous in her petitions; taking her prayer-book, she devoutly recited the prayers for the time of war, in which this supplication occurs:

"Build Thou up a wall around us, that the enemy may not approach our habitation."

When she had ended, the proprietor of the farm remarked that he thought that was asking too much of almighty God, but the old woman shook her head.

Now it was midwinter, and the cold was excessively sharp. When the day dawned, the inmates of the house, on looking out, were astonished to find that the wind had driven the snow and piled it up to such a height by the side of the road, as actually to form a wall which effectually hid the farmhouse from view. The family was amazed at the extraordinary height of the snow-drift.

Thus they had been defended from any molestation on the part of the soldiers, who during the hours of darkness had marched along the road past the house.

Thus God often protects His servants by natural means without miraculous intervention, and thereby manifests His omnipotence.

The Edict

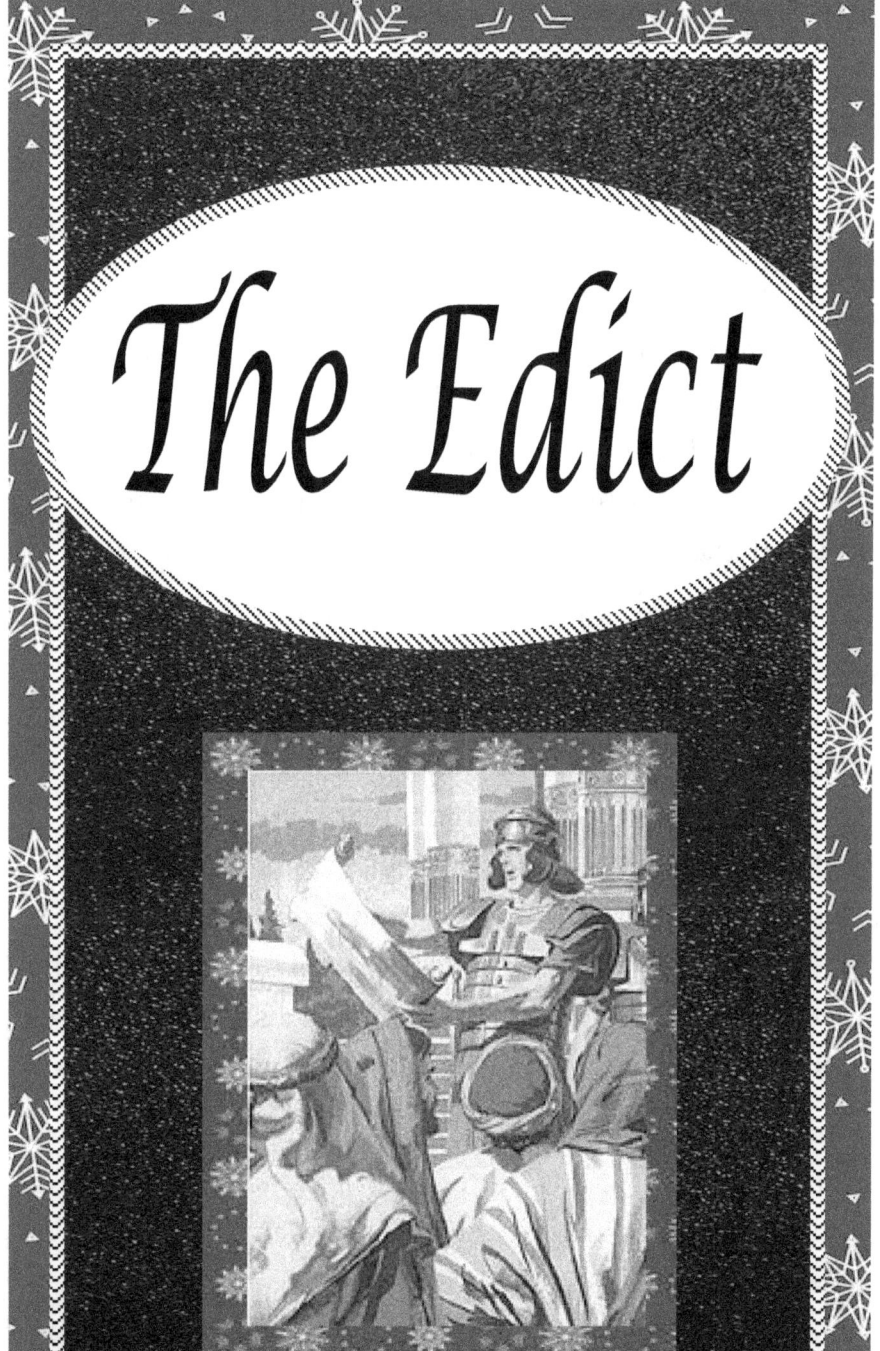

"God save us from the Romans!"

"Why must we go to the city of our fathers?"

"What is it all about?"

"Oh, the cruel Roman emperor!"

"What a hard journey!"

It had been many a long day since the little village of Nazareth was so excited. Small groups gathered here and there along the main street of the town, talking loudly. Women came rushing to windows and doors to learn the cause of the noise and excitement.

The men of the town were just returning after having heard the reading of the Roman emperor's latest command. He wanted to find out just how many subjects he had, so he had ordered the people of the whole country to go to the city from which their fathers had come, and there have their names placed upon the lists. These lists would then be counted and the results sent to him. He did not care if the people had to walk ten miles or fifty miles. Neither did he think of the many hardships that he was forcing upon them.

It was no wonder that the quiet people of Nazareth were excited. Of course, a few of them looked upon their journey with pleasure, because it gave them a chance to meet their friends and relatives. For most of them, however, the order meant a long, weary trip filled with hardships.

There was one man who did not linger with the

crowds. He was Joseph, the carpenter. The news saddened him very much, but he thought to himself, "It is the law and must be obeyed." He feared to tell his wife Mary the bad news, but when she heard the order of the emperor she said mildly, "We shall obey."

Plans were quickly made. The people gathered in small groups. In each group there were several donkeys to carry the little children, the women, and the food. Those going toward the west went in one group, those going toward the south in another. Among those traveling south were Joseph and Mary. They were going to Bethlehem, because they both belonged to the family of David, the great king who was born in Bethlehem.

It was a long, tiresome journey for Mary, even though she rode most of the way on one of the donkeys. Riding a donkey over a rough, stony road is not a pleasant thing. But she never complained. When Joseph thought that she was tired, he would drop from the company and rest with her along the roadside. Some of the friends who left Nazareth with Joseph and Mary withdrew from the group as they passed through the towns of their families. Others joined the company as it went from town to town. When the tired travelers beheld the gray walls of the city of Bethlehem rising from the top of a distant hill, the men cheered with joy. The end of a long and weary journey was in view. They hastened their steps, in order to arrive in the town before nightfall. *(Story continues with 'In Bethlehem'.)*

In Bethlehem

The sun had already disappeared behind the hills and a cold evening breeze was blowing when the travelers reached the gates of Bethlehem. The gathering shades of twilight had grown deeper and deeper. A prayer of thanks rose from the weary hearts. They had come to the end of the journey.

Bethlehem was all astir. There seemed to be crowds of people everywhere. Men, women, and children were talking and laughing, as they walked down the main street or gathered here and there in small groups. Friends and relatives who saw each other for the first time in years made the town ring with joy and mirth.

How could the little town hold all the people? Never before had such large numbers of men, women, and children passed through its gates. There were no great hotels nor large houses for the visitors. Many had made plans to spend the night in the homes of relatives or friends. Those who could not do this sought a place in the inn or little hotel. Very soon, however, the owner sent a message through the town, saying that he had no more room.

The pilgrims from distant Nazareth had arrived late. They hastened to the inn, but found no place to stay. The little group scattered in search of places to spend the night. Each family went its own way to find shelter.

The wintry winds that blew across the city were cold, sharp, and biting. Saint Joseph wrapped the Blessed

Virgin's shawl closely around her to protect her from the chilly air. She remained near the gates of the city while Joseph went in search of a place for her. Up and down the streets he went, knocking at every door and begging a place for Mary. As he passed from door to door, he always received the same answer, "We have no more room."

Poor Saint Joseph was tired. His heart was heavy and sad. He did not think of himself but he thought of his dearly beloved Mary. He must find a home for her. He took the few coins that he had, and offered them at house after house. Many of the people of the town became angry and slammed the door in his face. Some of the kind people who saw Mary near the gate tried to find a home for her, but the task was hopeless.

Joseph was sorry for Mary when he saw that the darkness of night had settled over the town and he had found no place for her. He did not mind the insults which had been heaped upon him. But it grieved him to tell Mary that nobody wanted them because they were so poor. The humble homes of Bethlehem little knew that they were turning the Lord of heaven and earth out into the cold world.

Almost in despair, Joseph approached a group of men standing near the gates of the city. He asked them if they knew of any place where Mary might spend the night. They had heard the same request from so many others that they paid no attention to it. But an old, old story tells of a little boy of twelve years who heard Joseph speak to the men. He noticed the sad and disappointed look on Joseph's face, and saw about the head of Mary a strange light that made her appear very beautiful. He shyly walked up to Joseph, and told him of a cave near the foot of a hill beyond the city gates.

These were the first kind words that Joseph had heard since his arrival in Bethlehem. It was now very dark, and Joseph did not know the way to the cave. The good boy was glad to go with him. Joseph placed Mary on the donkey. He led the tired animal by the halter, while the little boy walked ahead of them with a lantern in his hand. It seemed that Joseph's and Mary's only friends were the little boy and the stars twinkling above them. The story says that Jesus rewarded this boy for his kindness by giving him the gift of faith, and that later He called him to serve as a priest at the altar of God.

Joseph and Mary entered the cave. How dark, damp, and cold it was! Joseph raised his lantern to look around. The cave was just a large room carved out of rock. From cracks here and there, could be heard the continual drip, drip, drip of the water as it fell upon the ground. In one corner was the manger – a rather large hole cut in the rock, where clean hay and straw were kept. Here Mary sat down to rest. In another part of the cave, an ox lay, quietly eating some hay. Joseph placed his donkey near the ox, and soon all was silent, without and within.

About midnight, the cave suddenly brightened with a golden light. A sweet odour like perfume filled the air. The joyful music of angel voices was heard; for in that cave, Jesus, the Infant Saviour, was born. The Lord God of heaven and earth came into the world as a tiny Babe in the cave at Bethlehem.

Joseph knelt in silent adoration before the Holy Child. Mary kissed her Child again and again with all the tenderness of a fond mother's love. The joy of heaven was in her heart as she gazed into the sweet face of the Infant Jesus. He was her Child and she loved Him as her Son and her God.

Now, the Blessed Virgin had no lovely crib in which to place her little Babe and she had no pretty clothes to give Him. So she wrapped Him up in swaddling clothes and placed Him in the manger. Yes, a manger filled with straw in a cold, damp cave was the cradle of the Infant Jesus. A large cave dug in the side of a hill, a place without doors or windows, a shelter where the farmer kept his cows, was the first home of the Baby Jesus. How poor, how humble it was!

"The night is so cold," said Mary. "What shall I do to keep little Jesus warm?" She had already taken the shawl from her own shoulders and wrapped the Christ Child in it. But still He seemed cold. Just then the ox and the donkey walked over to the manger. They knelt before it and warmed the Holy Child with their breath. Sinful men had no place for Him in their homes in Bethlehem, but the ox and the donkey welcomed Him in their cave.

(Story continues with 'Waiting for the Saviour.')

Waiting for the Saviour

For hundreds and hundreds of years, the world had been waiting for the coming of Christ, the Saviour. Many stories had been told about Him by the prophets and the leaders of the Jewish people. Again and again, in the temple, the people had listened to the priests as they spoke about the Redeemer Who would come to save them.

Some thought that Christ would come as a great and glorious king. Others believed that He would come as a powerful general with a large army, to drive the Romans from the land of Israel. They all hoped that the great day would soon arrive when they would go forth to meet the Saviour of the people.

Little did they think that the Saviour would come as a tiny, poor, helpless Babe. Little did they dream that the Redeemer would be born in a cave, with no one to welcome Him. The Jews were looking for a Saviour surrounded with riches, pomp, and glory – one they could greet with cheers and songs of praise.

But the ways of God are not like the ways of men. Our heavenly Father wanted to teach the world a lesson in humility that it would never forget. Therefore, He sent His divine Son into the world as an outcast, born of a poor but holy Virgin in a cold, dreary cave. No servants bowed before Him ready to obey His wishes. No great heralds with silver trumpets announced His coming in the marble palaces of the rich or in the great churches. No royal edict told the world of the birth of Christ, the King.

On that first Christmas night, God looked down from His throne in heaven. He saw shepherds with their flocks on the hillsides outside the city of Bethlehem. These were good, simple, honest men who spent their days and nights with their sheep. They loved their sheep, and the sheep loved them. They guarded them very carefully from the attacks of roaming wild beasts. Sometimes hungry wolves would lie still in the forests all day, and at night sneak out to the sheepfold, and carry a little lamb away to the woods. Therefore, during the night one shepherd always kept watch while the others slept.

It was a peaceful scene that God looked upon. The sleeping sheep were huddled together, and in the moonlight appeared like a rolling field of gray. Now and then, flames leaped from the camp fires and showed the faces of tired shepherds who dozed upon the ground wrapped in blankets. One silent form slowly wandered about the sheepfold. It was the shepherd on watch.

God thought to Himself that He would make known the birth of the Saviour to these poor honest men first. He sent His angels with the glad news. The shepherds were suddenly roused by a dazzling, bright light. Trembling in fear, they gazed at one another. The frightened men wondered what was going to happen. The sheep thought that morning had come and greeted it with their gentle bleating. *(Story continues with 'The Message from Heaven.')*

The Message from Heaven

The shepherds gathered together to help and protect one another. The sky above them seemed to have opened, letting fall a shower of golden brightness upon the earth. Soon a beautiful angel, shining in glory, was seen standing in the bright light. The angel noticed how frightened the poor shepherds were, so he spoke in a kind, low voice. "Fear not," he said, "for behold, I bring you good tidings of great joy that shall be to all the people. For this day is born to you a Saviour, who is Christ the Lord, in the city of David. And this shall be a sign unto you: you shall find the Infant wrapped in swaddling clothes and laid in a manger."

The shepherds thought that they were dreaming. The Lord and Saviour born in Bethlehem? Yes, they had all heard it. While they were still wondering, a great number of angels appeared in the sky, praising God and singing,

"Glory to God in the highest; and on earth, peace to men of good will."

Such sweet music had never before been heard on earth. It was God's own choir. Then fainter and fainter the voices sounded, as the angels faded in the deep blue sky.

When the blackness of night returned, and the music of the angels had died away in the distance, the shepherds stood in silence. Then they said, "Let us go over to Bethlehem, and let us see this word that is come to pass, which the Lord has shown us." In their eagerness they did not wait for morning, but immediately hastened over the hill to the cave where they found Mary and Joseph watching over the Infant Jesus lying in the manger.

They told Joseph and Mary about the message of the angel and the beautiful choir from heaven that God had sent to announce the birth of Jesus. They knelt in prayer before the tiny Infant in the manger, adoring Him as their God and Saviour.

The shepherds lost no time in spreading the startling news throughout the town of Bethlehem. The birth of Christ the Lord was made known to all they met. The people wondered at the stories about the angels told by the shepherds from the hills.

The Lady in White

The cold winds from the mountain sent a chill through the simple cottages in the little town of Lourdes. The good housewives poked the fires in the open hearths and threw short logs into the flames. In one of the little homes, the dying fire was poked but there was no wood to put into it.

"Bernadette," called the housewife, "go with your sister to the forest near the river and get some wood. The howling of that sharp wind tells me that it is going to be a cold night."

Bernadette, a girl of fourteen, went with her sister and a playmate to gather the dry branches that fell by the river. The girls enjoyed the cold wind against their faces. They darted here, there, and everywhere, seeing who could find the most wood. In their eagerness, two of the girls waded through the shallow stream and wandered far into the forest.

Bernadette was left behind. She was not as strong as the others and therefore had to go more slowly. As she approached the bank of the river, she was startled by a rustling sound in a grotto on the side of a hill near her. She looked around and saw a bush swaying as if blown by the wind. Then in the grotto above the bush appeared a bright golden light. The little child gazed in surprise.

Little by little, the bright light faded away, and there in the grotto stood a beautiful woman, smiling sweetly at the little peasant girl. Bernadette had never seen a more lovely face. She had heard stories about holy saints and fairy godmothers, but she had never dreamed of anything so pretty as the Lady in White.

In her long white robe, the lady stood like a statue. A girdle of pale blue was tied about her waist, and the ends fell gracefully at the left side. Over her head and shoulders and down her back was draped a white veil. A rosary with a golden cross was placed upon her left arm. Her hands were folded piously at her breast. Her tender eyes gazed sadly yet sweetly upon the world.

Little Bernadette fell upon her knees. She knew that the beautiful woman must have come from heaven. She folded her tiny hands in prayer, never taking her eyes from the silent figure in white that stood in the rock grotto.

The vision grew dimmer and dimmer, until the lovely lady disappeared.

The little child was still kneeling in prayer when her playmates returned with their arms filled with wood. They wondered what was the matter with Bernadette. They had never seen her praying in the woods before.

"Bernadette," they said, "see all the wood we found. Where is your wood?" Bernadette was ashamed that she had not gathered more wood for her mother. She was also sorry that the girls had found her praying. She wanted to keep her vision a secret. Gathering up the few pieces of wood she had found, she joined her playmates on their homeward journey.

But Bernadette's secret made her so happy that she could not keep it. She whispered it to her sister, and her sister whispered it to her mother. That night when the flames were dancing in the open fireplace, the little family talked about the Lady in White who had appeared at the grotto.

Time and again, the lovely Lady appeared to the holy peasant girl. The story was soon carried far and wide. Men, women, and children from all the near-by towns hurried to the grotto to see the vision. Many believed and many doubted.

Once as Bernadette knelt in prayer before the grotto, the Lady appeared to her and beckoned her to climb the rocks. With her eyes fastened on the vision, Bernadette started up the rocks.

In a sweet, clear voice, the Lady told her to wash in the water at her feet. The little child looked around but could see no water. With her hands, she dug a small hole in the ground, and a stream of water bubbled forth. The people who had gathered at the small grotto gazed in amazement. They knew that there had been no spring or water near the spot before.

At another time, the Lady in White told Bernadette to have a chapel built there in her honor and to have people go in procession to it. This was indeed no easy task. But God saw to it that the chapel was built, and people from all over the world have gone to it in large processions.

Each year, trains bring thousands and thousands of sick, blind, deaf, and lame to Lourdes to seek a cure. They pray before the shrine of the Lady in White and bathe in the pools that are filled with water from Bernadette's spring. Each year, the sick are cured, the blind see, the deaf hear, and the lame walk.

It is God's way of rewarding them for their faith, and of showing the wonderful power of the Lady in White.

And who was the Lady in White that appeared to Bernadette?

When the little girl asked the Lady her name, she said, "I AM THE IMMACULATE CONCEPTION." She was the holy Mother of God who was always free from any stain of sin. It was Mary, then, the Blessed Virgin, the Mother of Jesus, who appeared to Bernadette in the grotto at Lourdes, and it is through her help that the wonderful miracles are performed at Lourdes today.

The Frozen Hands

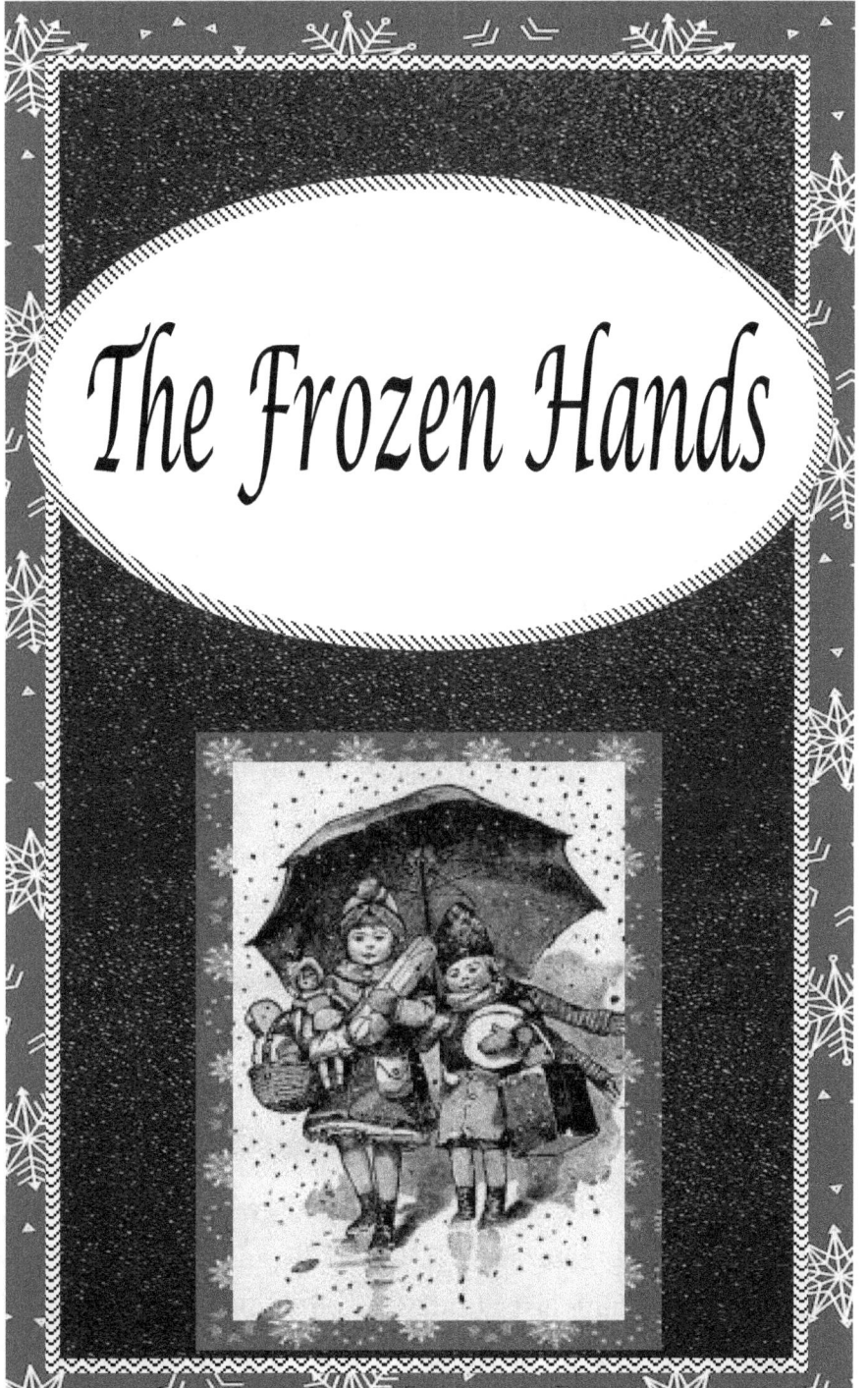

The Princess Gerda and her little brother were playing in their nursery one afternoon in the winter-time, when the snow lay on the ground and icicles hung from every tree, and the wind was so bitterly cold that the children were not allowed to go out.

"Oh, look, Ivan," cried the little Princess, as she looked out of the window into the castle yard. "See the poor children!"

"Our father will see that they are given money," said Ivan; "he has ordered the servants never to turn anyone away from the door."

"I wish we could go down and speak to them," said Gerda. "We never do anything for the poor, and yet our grandmother belonged to the same family as Queen Elizabeth of Hungary, who was so good to the poor that she worked miracles."

"Well," returned the Prince, "I have a plan in my head, and if you will promise not to tell it to nurse, as you generally do, I will tell you."

"Oh, Ivan, I promise faithfully, and I never told any of your secrets when you made me promise not to."

"Come into the corner, then," said Ivan, drawing into a corner of the big nursery. "Did you listen to Father Nickanor preaching last Sunday, and did you hear what he said about helping those in need? Well, we too must do something for the poor this winter."

"But what shall we do? We are never allowed to go out alone."

"We shall go out on Christmas Eve, when everybody is in church, and Caterina has left us here alone. You must sew some clothes by that time, instead of always making clothes for your dolls, and we must get the cook to give us some food. We can give all the money Grandmother has given us on our birthdays, too."

"Yes," agreed Gerda cheerfully, although she disliked sewing very much. "But, oh, Ivan, have you thought how dark it will be, and the wolves? I heard one howling last Christmas night, when I was in bed."

"Well, of course, if you are going to be afraid, I must go by myself," answered Ivan, rather crossly. "You are always talking about the poor, so I thought you would be brave enough for that."

"Yes, I will go, Ivan dear," said the little girl, putting her arms around her brother's neck, "and I will begin the sewing tomorrow."

Every day the little Princess sat sewing for the poor children when she and Ivan were not at lessons or out walking in the grounds with Caterina or sleighing.

Towards Christmas Eve their father and mother went to spend Christmas at the Court of the Czar. You know, they belonged to the Czar's court, so they had to go each year for the big celebration that was held.

Ivan and Gerda were quite free to carry out their little plans, as Caterina did not trouble very much about them when the Princess Mother was away.

On Christmas Eve, when they were sure everyone was in church at confession, they dressed themselves in their warm furs.

Then they filled a large basket with the clothes that Princess Gerda had made and with the good things they had coaxed from the cook. When all was ready, they carried the basket downstairs, opened the door, and looked out.

It was a bitterly cold night, and the snow lay deep on the ground. The moon was bright and many beautiful stars filled the sky.

"Oh!" shivered Gerda, as they stepped out into the cold.

"Now, then," said Ivan, "are you going to be a baby?"

"No," answered Gerda, but her voice shook.

The moon lighted up the snow until it shone with dazzling brightness, but the shadows cast by the trees and bushes were very dark. What awful thing, thought the little Princess, might not be hidden in the darkness, ready to spring out and pounce upon them as they passed.

"Come on," said the Prince, as they passed by a little cluster of fir trees, "let us hasten, or perhaps Caterina will notice that we are gone, and will come after us."

To tell the truth, he was beginning to be rather afraid himself, but he was ashamed to have his sister know that.

"We can't go any faster with this heavy basket," gasped Gerda. "Change hands with me, Ivan." Her poor little hands were fast becoming numbed.

They trudged on for about a mile, and then found themselves on the top of a hill, at the foot of which was the village. They could hear the Christmas bells and see the lights of torches which the people going to church carried in their hands.

"There," said Ivan joyfully, as they put down the basket to rest for a moment; "we have gone more than half the way."

But it was very difficult going down the hill with the heavy basket. It was so slippery that every now and then they slid down a few steps, which ended in a fall. Gerda lost one of her snow-shoes, and Ivan bruised his head very badly in a fall.

"Shall we ever get there?" sobbed Gerda, her little shoeless foot hurting her dreadfully with the cold. "My hands and my foot are freezing, Ivan, and they will drop off."

"So are mine," answered Ivan. "What shall we do if our hands freeze to the basket?"

Gerda sobbed louder than ever, and even Ivan's tears flowed. They were so cold and tired that their courage disappeared.

"Let us pray to the Infant Jesus," said Gerda. "He will not let us freeze so, when we came out on purpose to please Him."

They knelt down and prayed together:

"Jesus, sweetest Infant, born in a stable, laid in a manger, crucified on the hard wood of the cross, help us in our hour of need." It was a little prayer their mother had taught them, and Gerda added to it:

"And please keep our hands from freezing to the basket, dear Jesus."

Then they took up their basket, but it seemed to have grown so light that they cried out in wonder.

"You have let some of the things drop out," said Ivan.

"No; it is just as full up to the brim as when we started; and, see, the things are in the same place," said Gerda, lifting a corner of the wolf-skin with which they had covered their treasures. "And, oh!" she cried, "I am quite warm, and the snow feels like a warm bear-skin to my foot, and my hands are like toast."

"So are mine," exclaimed Ivan joyfully. "It is Jesus, Who has answered our prayers. So let us kneel and thank Him from the bottom of our hearts."

They knelt on the snow, which now felt warm to them, and thanked God for helping them.

As they went on down the hill, the snow still felt warm to their feet, and the basket light to carry.

In the first cottage they entered, they found an old woman in bed. She was so very, very old that she shivered with the cold, though there was a large fire burning on the hearth. They covered her with a warm blanket which Gerda had knitted, and she immediately cried out that she no longer felt the cold, and her teeth stopped chattering, and her stiffened fingers grew warm so that she could move them.

The two children passed on through the village giving something from the basket to all the needy ones. There was no one in want who did not receive the very thing he needed most.

At last they came to a hut in which they found a little lame boy. He had not been able to walk, or even move about, for nine years. Gerda gave him the best and nicest things from the cook's store and, putting her little arms around his neck, she kissed him. Immediately the little lame boy felt the pain in his back vanish. He got up and ran to meet his mother, who had just returned from Mass and Communion, and had been praying to the Infant Jesus for her little son.

After a long time, the two children were missed from the castle. Caterina guessed they must have gone out into the streets, for she found their little coats and hats were missing. With the other servants she started out to look for them. When she at last found them, at the other end of the village, she was too relieved to scold, so the two little ones were bundled into the big sleigh and driven home. There had been time, however, for the little runaways to make sad hearts glad.

To this day, in that small village, the fathers and mothers tell their children on Christmas Eve the story of the little Prince and Princess who set out on that day with a large basket of food and clothing in honour of the Infant Jesus. And they never forgot to tell how the dear Jesus helped the little ones when their poor little hands were freezing and how He rewarded their devotion by the miraculous cure of the lame boy.

Piccola

How happy was little Piccola! Busy was little Piccola! Her father was often away from home fishing far out at sea. Then she and her mother were left all alone in their little stone cottage, in a small village in France.

Piccola helped keep the cottage clean; she scoured the pots and pans; she tended the geraniums that bloomed in the windows; she dragged in great armfuls of wood for the fire.

"My little Piccola is as busy as the bee," said her mother.

"My little Piccola is as happy as the lark," said her father.

When her work was done, Piccola raced with the other children through the narrow streets of the village, her little wooden shoes going rat-a-tat-too on the cobblestones, or she climbed up high on the rocks that rose behind the town and looked far out to sea where the sailboats danced in the breeze.

"A jolly good comrade is Piccola," her little playmates said.

But one year, when the yellowed leaves fell from the trees, and the snow began to fall, there came to Piccola's home a time of sadness. Poor had the fishing season been the summer before, and the good father had laid little money by to meet their needs for the winter. He came in from the stormy sea, to go out no more till the spring returned, and he could get no work to earn money through the winter.

"I do not know how we shall ever get on until spring," he mourned.

But Piccola was none the less happy.

"God gives us our daily bread," she said, and her little heart was grateful for each day's simple food.

As the weeks slipped by, and their little store of money grew smaller and smaller, the Christmas-tide drew near.

"What shall we do for Piccola?" said the mother, "we are so poor, we cannot buy her even one small gift."

"No," said her father, "not even one small gift."

Piccola's Christmas

Now close by the church, past which Piccola often romped in her play, there stood a mass of old gray stone, carved with quaint figures that told of the life of Jesus. Stiff and queerly fashioned were the figures, but they had been carved by those who loved the story, and Piccola loved it too. As she carefully traced out all the tale, she said to herself full of reverence:

"It was Jesus who taught men to know the good God as their Father, to let His Goodness shine in their hearts, and to love one another."

So when the Christ-mass drew near and men made ready to celebrate the coming of Jesus Christ to men, Piccola had no thought but that all the earth must rejoice.

"I love the good Christmas-tide!" she cried.

"But, Piccola," said her mother, "do you not know that no gifts can come to you this year?"

"Good gifts must come to all with Christmas," the child made answer, simply.

"Poor little one," said the mother in a low voice to the father, "if we only had one sou to spare to buy her the least little gift."

So the father and mother were sorrowful, but Piccola was happy.

On the night before Christmas, Piccola sang as she swept up the hearth, and when her share of the evening's work was done, she seized her father and mother each by the hand.

"Let us go out and be merry!" she cried.

So they left their dingy little cottage and went out into the village. All the windows were ablaze with light, and hung with festoons and gay Christmas baubles. So close to the street were the little stone houses, that Piccola and her mother and father could see all the happiness and cheer within.

"Every house but ours is happy," said the father. But

Piccola did not even hear him. She was laughing with joy at the joy she saw. Every joyful festoon, every joyful Christmas bauble, all the happiness and cheer in every house they passed was hers to enjoy! She was far richer than those who had only one cottage with festooned windows!

So they went on to the very last house in the village. There they saw three little children carefully setting their wooden shoes by the fireplace, to be filled with Christmas gifts.

"Tomorrow they will be full of goodies!"

"And full of toys!" rang their shrill little voices.

"I shall set out my shoe too!" cried Piccola with shining eyes.

"Piccola, there can be no Christmas gifts for you!" her mother repeated half sobbing. But still Piccola did not hear. Too firm was her faith that every child shared alike in the love of the good God, and none could be shut out from receiving His good gifts.

By the dim candle light she made ready for bed. In her heart was all the joy of the merriment she had seen in the village. Last of all she set by the hearth, where the fire was dying down, her little wooden shoe.

"Through all the year, I have been as good as I know how," she cried, "so I shall find something good here tomorrow."

Then Piccola crept happily into bed, but her mother and father sat long by the embers, and looked sorrowfully at the waiting shoe they had no gifts to fill.

Slowly the night wore away and the gray dawn came. Piccola opened her eyes.

"Christmas is come!" she cried and sprang from her bed. Eagerly, expectantly, she crept to her little shoe.

Her mother and father heard her, and listened with bated breath. "Another minute," they thought, "and she will cry out in disappointment!"

But joyfully on the air, rang a sound of gladness.

"See! Oh, see! My shoe is full!"

Astonished, Father and Mother hurried into the room. There stood Piccola with shining face, caressing her shoe, and cozily resting in it, lay — a bright-eyed little bird.

"It fell down the chimney and into her shoe!" her father said; but Piccola did not heed him. The bird had come as her Christmas gift, she knew. And every wish of her heart was satisfied and fulfilled. All day long she warmed the bird, and cuddled it, and fed it, till at last her father and mother, seeing how happy she was, caught her joy and were happy, too.

So Christmas came to Piccola rich and full, because Christmas was always in her heart.

Florence's Christmas

Yes, there's happiness in goodness, if there's happiness anywhere. Within the hidden sweetness of a good deed there lurks a joy - not, indeed, of earth, but of heaven. God, infinitely good, is also infinitely happy. Oh, for an unceasing round of little deeds of kindness and little words of love!

All this Florence Cimmon experienced of a beautiful Christmas morning. "Merry Christmas!" was on the lips of all. The densely-filled cars bore it along, the hurrying crowds scattered it with profuse cheerfulness. "Merry Christmas! Merry Christmas!" Florence stood at the parlor window of her neat little home on Hancock Street and gazed upon the scene of Yuletide merriment. She was all dressed and ready for church - St. John's was only six blocks away. How very happy she seemed to be! Surely, it was because of Mass, Communion, and the Crib—for what is like a Christmas Mass, what like Christmas Communion with its blissful thanksgiving, before the Omnipotent Babe of the Crib? Or were her thoughts happily occupied with Christmas gifts, with sweets and goodies, all encircling a fragrant tree? Oh, no. In years gone by they, too, had seemed to make her joy more full, but today Florence had neither gifts nor tree. She had them not, because she loved Christ's poor.

"Mother," she had said three days before, "Sister Mary told us today of Jesus' poor, of those little ones who have naught for Christmas. Many, she said, will have a lone and dreary Christmas; no presents, no sweets, no Christmas dinner, not even Christmas joys. To give to such as these, she told us, would be to place a gift into the very hands of the smiling Christ-Child. Mother dear, please, oh please, pack all my gifts and my sweets away—distribute them among the poor mothers of Harcot's Lane. The boys and girls, you know, are all awaiting the Christ-Child's coming. How happy they will then be—how bitterly disappointed otherwise! Mother, I want nothing—I want only Jesus and His love—I want to give something to Jesus. Come, now, mother, won't you, dear?"

How very pleased her mother had been! "But, Florence, would you really like it? Would you be truly happy?"

"Oh, yes," she had answered. "I could not otherwise be happy. In the Crib little Jesus stretches out His baby hands to me. Can I say no to Him? Oh, I cannot, I may not, nor do I wish to do so. Never fear, I'll be happy, Mother; I'll get more than the whole world, with all its holy Christmas joys: Jesus in Holy Communion."

And so it was Christmas morning, and Florence was without the usual books and parcels and goodies and without a Christmas tree. It seemed strange indeed; yet still more strange, was the pure and happy sensation which gently thrilled her through and through. She was more light-hearted and cheery than she had ever been before. 'Twas happiness in goodness—only this she knew.

And at St. John's the Mass was—oh, so wonderful!

Father Hubert's voice trembled with holy emotion at the angelic "Gloria in excelsis Deo." How the organ pealed in accompaniment to a mighty volume of stirring song! And then her Communion—never had it been so full of rapture and sweetness, never had Jesus spoken so tenderly to her loving heart. He seemed to come to her a little child, to kiss her with soft baby lips, to cling to her confidingly with His tiny arms.

After Mass she knelt long and devoutly before the Crib, almost hidden as it was in a miniature evergreen grove. Her heart was well-nigh bursting with gratitude. "My Infant Saviour, sweetest, gentlest Jesus," she whispered softly, "I've never been so happy before. Oh, how can I ever thank You? Dear Christ Child, I have all my Christmas gifts in You."

Still burning with love and full of happiness found in goodness, Florence returned home about thirty minutes later. What was her surprise to find nearly all the boys and girls of Harcot's Lane awaiting her. "Merry Christmas! Merry Christmas!" Again and again, amid the ring of joyous laughter, the hearty greetings were exchanged. A Christmas tree all ablaze with lights and a-glimmer with tinsel stood in the center of the parlor. Ruddy apples and yellow oranges glowed among the odorous branches of green. And what a heap of bags and bundles, of books and games and whatnot there was at the bottom! Florence was amazed.

She looked at the smiling faces of her happy young friends, knowing not whether to laugh or to cry—to cry out of sheer joy. But just then her mother and Uncle John entered the room—wealthy Uncle John, the Broadway banker. He smiled at Florence's surprise and bewilderment. Then turning to her mother he said: "Tell her all about it, Mary."

"My dearest Florence," said her mother, and she accompanied these words with a kiss, "on Christmas Eve I told Uncle John of your wish to give all your gifts to the children of Harcot's Lane. Now, you know, Uncle John loves both the poor and the lovers of the poor. So he played the part of the bountiful Christ Child in their regard. He made this Christmas one which will ever be remembered by your young friends here as the very happiest of their lives. Yes, he simply heaped the choicest of gifts and the most useful presents upon them. More than this, he bade them bring this beautiful tree and all these pretty things to you. Now, dressed in their best, they have come to make your Christmas the happiest of the happy; the merriest of the merry. Florence dear, there's truly happiness in goodness, isn't there?"

"So, my dear children," she added, addressing the shining faces round her, "laugh and chat and sing and feast all day long. Now for a Christmas breakfast, then for a Christmas dinner! 'Peace on earth, to men of good will' - peace and joy."

"You see, Florence," said Uncle John with one of his big, hearty smiles, "the Child Jesus has already given back all that you gave Him, hasn't He?"

"Oh, a thousand times more," murmured Florence. She was thinking of the joy of giving. Wasn't it greater than the joy of receiving—although that, too, was very great?

Saint Lucy

The silver gloom of a Roman twilight was settling over the snow-clad hill, and the wind had blown the flakes into drifts to hide the path. One arm about her mother, who seemed too frail for the weary climb, a girl of fourteen was making her way slowly toward the summit. Outlined against the gray skies above them, stood the white tomb of Saint Agatha.

Even as a little child, Lucy had loved Agatha's story, and had prayed that she too might one day die for Jesus' sake. Now for long years her mother had been ill, and doctors had been unable to cure her.

Lucy had thought of the girl saint. Would not Jesus listen to her prayer, since she had died for Him? With new hope in their hearts, the girl and her mother had set out for Saint Agatha's tomb, there to plead for health.

The mother's face was lined with pain, yet she smiled when the girl turned to her with a word of love or merry little jest.

"It is not far now, my mother," Lucy cried; "see, there it lies above us, half buried in the snow." The child's eyes, gentle and meek as those of a dove, were lifted in confidence to the shaft of gray stone gleaming through the bare trees, and her courage inspired the poor mother to a last strong effort.

Following her daughter's gaze, she looked up the steep ascent, trying to forget the rugged toil some way, in the hope that the little tomb seemed to promise. A few moments, and perhaps the pain of a lifetime would be forgotten.

"I see it, child," she answered; "with God's help we will reach it before night fall."

With fresh courage they pressed on, and weary, but full of joy, reached the little tomb.

The snow fell more softly now, and the wind had died away. A strange peace seemed to hover over the white -robed earth. Near to the tomb was a tumbled hut, and within its poor walls the mother and daughter sought a little rest. As Lucy slept, her head pillowed against the rough boards, in a dream she saw Saint Agatha. The martyr's robe was shining like the starlight, and her arms were outstretched in joyous welcome. "Lucy, my sister," she whispered, "your mother will be cured."

Even in her sleep Lucy felt the happiness that surged through her soul at that glad message, but her heart almost ceased beating as Agatha stooped and gathered her in her arms. A wave of longing to be with God swept over her, a stronger, purer love for Him than she had ever felt before.

"Little sister," Agatha said, and her voice was trium-phant with gladness, "Jesus has heard your prayer. The crown of martyrdom shall be yours."

"Thank God, thank God," Lucy sobbed, and with that sweet cry on her lips, awoke to find her mother standing before her in the morning sunlight, cured of her infirmity.

The days that followed were joyous ones for Lucy. All that she had she gave to the poor, and over and over again promised the dear Lord to live for Him alone until she might lay her life in sacrifice at His feet.

The time was not far distant. A persecution of the Christians was even then raging, and soon Lucy was brought before the prefect. She was condemned to be burned alive, but when she was cast into the flames God saved her from the heat. Then it was ordered that her heart should be pierced with a sword. And so, on the thirteenth of December, soon after the vision at the tomb of Saint Agatha, her soul sped forth to God.

Her feast day is December thirteenth.

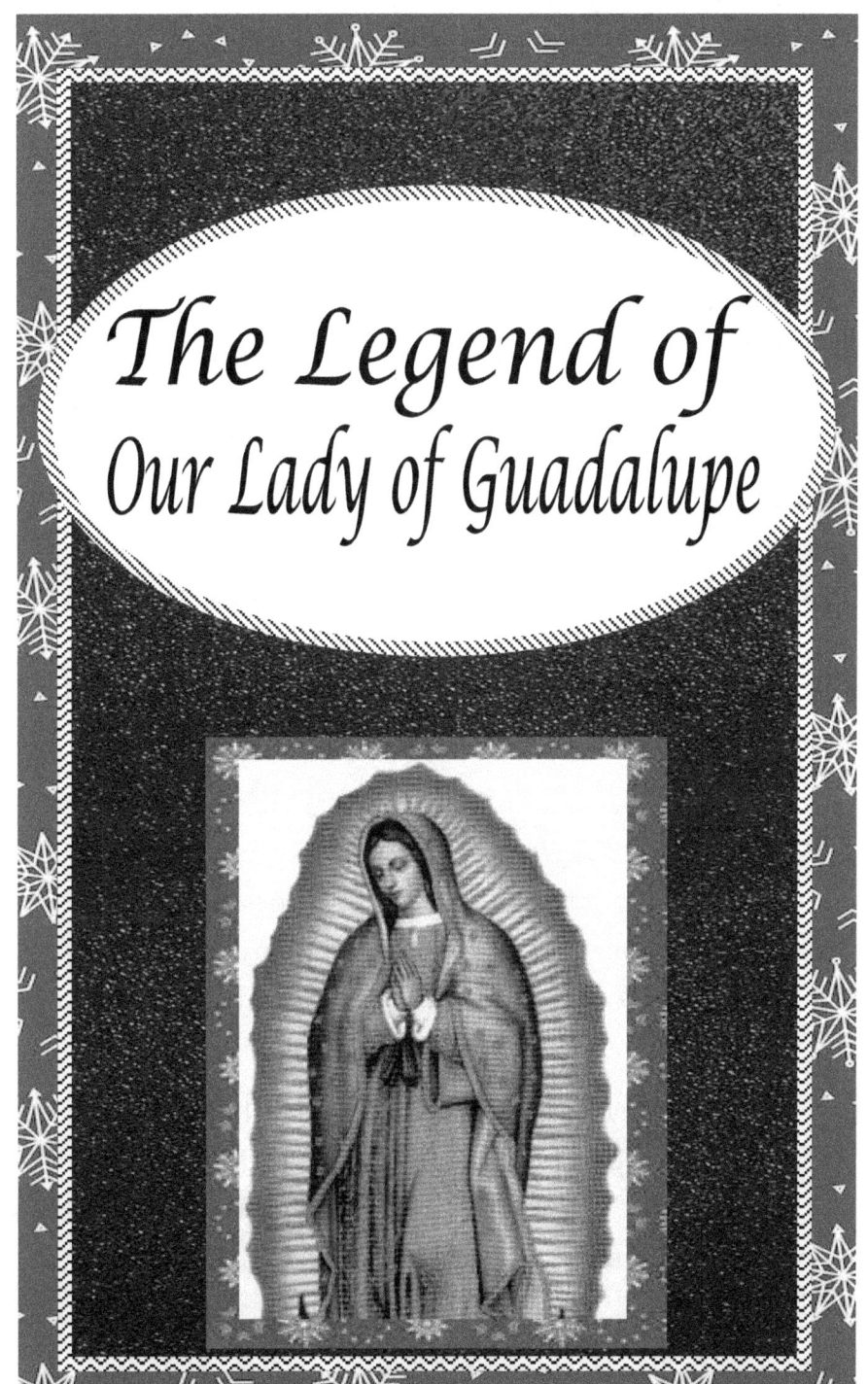

The Legend of
Our Lady of Guadalupe

Strangers had been amongst the Indian tribes, strangers who showed them no mercy, who drove them from their dwellings like hunted deer; and there was none to help them, for when they called upon their heathen god he did not heed their prayer.

But holy men came through the forest paths, who told them of God and the Blessed Virgin, and taught them to live as Christian men. One of the noblest of the race made his dwelling there; he learned each tale the Fathers told of mercy, and every week he journeyed to the nearest city to hear Mass in her honour. On his way he passed a hill where a heathen temple had once stood, and there he would always pause and sing the litany of the Blessed Virgin, that the evil spirits might be put to flight if they still lingered there.

Once, while singing the praises of Mary on that hill-side, he heard sweet strains mixing with his own strains so sweet that he felt sure they came from no voice of this world and then, in the midst of dazzling light, a figure stood before him whom he knew to be the Queen of men and angels.

"I know thy love for me," she said, "therefore I bid thee to take a message to the chief of the holy Fathers: say to him that I will have thee raise a church upon this spot where I stand, and none shall invoke me here in vain."

The Indian hastened to the Bishop. He spoke of

the vision he had seen and of the desire of his glorious Mother; but the Father's words were cold and stern: "It is a wondrous tale," he said; "but I dare not think it true."

Again the chieftain heard the singing on the hillside, again he saw the dazzling light, while the sweet voice spoke to him: "Hast thou performed my will?" it said; and, bowed to the ground, he could only tell her it had been in vain; his message was not believed.

"Seek thy priest again," said the vision; "bid him, if he loves me, attend to my request." And the Indian went; but the Father only smiled: "Thou hast done what was bidden thee; go in peace," he said.

Sadly and sorrowfully the Indian went homeward. Our Lady stood before him once again, asking him of his success, and then she bid him return to her on the morrow, when he should bear a sign to the Bishop from her.

He went. The Blessed Virgin appeared, and, smiling, bid him bring flowers from the hillside, and with these she twined a fragrant wreath, which he should bear to the good Father, in token that the vision was true. The Indian wrapped his treasure in his cloak, and took his way through the city, where he sought the Bishop.

"See, my Father," he cried, "our Blessed Mother has sent to you a sign," and as he spoke he threw back the folds of his cloak. Ah! No flowers are there, no half-faded wreath, but the face of the Virgin Mother! Drawn as though by angels, before which the Bishop bent his knees in reverence. Multitudes came flocking to see that wondrous sign, and there, upon the hill top, a church was raised, in which there was an altar to Mary, blazing with gold and rarest gems, given by the chief of the Indians; and the cloak with its marvelous likeness was preserved as a sacred relic of the Mother of God, whose praises are sung by many thousands of Christian pilgrims to that spot.

The Christmas Kiss

The time? It was the morning of the day before Christmas. The place? Africa. The people? A group of dark-skinned children gathered round Sister in the little Catholic school near the mission church. Everybody was so busy getting ready for Christmas! There were the altars to be decorated, the crib to be arranged, and a thousand and one other things to be done. The children helped Sister as only little people can help at such a blessed time.

The dinner hour drew near. Then Sister said, "Go home now, darlings, and get your dinner. And remember, each one is going to give the Christ Child a present this afternoon, by bringing something to help decorate crib or church or altar."

Away they went, about fifteen of them, chatting eagerly and planning happily about what they should bring the Saviour in the afternoon. Only one tiny girl, Naga, a poor little orphan that was staying at the mission, was not happy. She had no pennies to buy decorations with; she had not even flowers to give. But as Naga's big black eyes watched the other children disappear, a look of joy suddenly sprang into her face—and she was unhappy no longer. She knew what she would do!

Sister noticed with joy that Naga was much more helpful and happy than usual that afternoon. The girl even lovingly helped the other children arrange their flowers and candles and similar gifts; she shared in their delight, though she had nothing to give herself. What did I say?

She had nothing to give? Oh, yes, she had! In her heart, she knew all the while just what she would give—and how.

Now, late in the afternoon Sister began to bake the altar breads for the coming day. Naga, of course, always helped—she loved that work more than any other. First Sister baked the large host for the Mass and placed it on a clean white cloth. Then she baked the smaller hosts for Holy Communion.

But what was Naga doing back there? Sister turned around just in time to see her reverently take the large host in both her little hands and giving it a long, sweet, lingering kiss.

"Why, Naga!" she exclaimed. "What are you doing? Didn't I tell you often that the unconsecrated host is only a little wafer of bread? It is not Jesus in the Blessed Sacrament until, during Mass, at the altar, the priest speaks over it the sacred words, 'This is My Body'."

"Oh Sister, I know. But it is my Christmas Gift to Jesus, my Christmas Kiss. I have nothing else to give Him, so I placed it upon the host in order that when He comes tomorrow, He may find it there. Did I do wrong, Sister?" And she gazed into Sister's face in innocent pleading.

"No, no," said Sister gently, as she lovingly drew the little darky girl's head to her breast, "you did no wrong, darling. He will surely find it there."

The next morning when the priest raised the Sacred Host aloft at the elevation, during the beautiful Christmas Mass, one little girl in church looked upon It with the love-light of heaven in her eyes. She knew He had found it.

Found it? What? Why, Naga's Christmas Kiss.

The Christmas Cloak

Jennie came home from school crying. It was only a few days before Christmas at that. Surely, no time for tears.

"What are you crying for, Jennie?" Mother asked anxiously.

"Oh, Mother, Marie has clothes so much nicer than mine," sobbed the girl.

"Now, Jennie, aren't you ashamed of yourself?" Mother said, surprised. "Is that the way to be a good girl, thinking about nice clothes even when you are in church? Your clothing is neat and warm, and you always have enough. What more do you want? You must thank God for taking such good care of us. And don't forget that Marie's father is rich. He can afford to buy her more expensive garments. But you know Father has to work hard every day to support us. While we have a comfortable home to live in and healthy food to eat, and warm clothes to wear, we should be grateful to God—and bless Him for keeping Father well and strong. Really, Jennie, it is very naughty of you to be dissatisfied."

Just then Mother saw Elsie Prull walking down the street. "See," she said, "there's Elsie. What a poor, thin cloak she wears! She is just shivering from the cold. But it's the best she has; for she is poor and her mother has been sick for a long time. And you, who have everything you need, and more even, are crying out of envy. Jennie, do you think God likes that?"

Now, Jennie was really a good girl, so she saw at once how wrong it was for her to act in such a way. Then too, there was Elsie—she pitied Elsie.

"Mother," she said suddenly, "I'm sorry I acted so thoughtlessly. I'm quite ashamed! And Mother—you know I have an extra cloak upstairs. It's warm and heavy and still good. Won't you let me give it to Elsie, please?"

How happy Mother was to hear that! Now her darling was a darling indeed. "Of course you may," she said. "Though we haven't much, we must not forget those who have even less."

At once Jennie hastened over to Elsie's home, a bundle under her arm. It was the cloak. Oh, how happy Elsie and her poor sick mother were! They were so happy that they cried.

That night Jennie had a dream. "Oh, Mother," she cried the next morning, "what a lovely dream I had last night. I dreamt I saw the Christ Child, just as He came to us the first Christmas night. Oh, He was so sweet and dear! He smiled upon me and stretched out His arms for me to come and kiss Him. And Mother—He had on my cloak—the one I gave to Elsie!" Jennie's eyes were moist with emotion and her voice trembled.

"See, Jennie, thus Jesus rewards you. Thus He shows you that what you do for others in His name you do for Him."

A few days later Christmas came. Under her beautiful tree Jennie found an extra large box. What could it be? She opened it. "Oh Mother," she cried, "see what the Christ Child brought me! A cloak, just like the one I gave away; only all new! Oh, Mother, it's just as though I gave it to Jesus, and He gave it back much nicer than before."

And in church that day, kneeling before the crib, Jennie whispered, "Dear Baby God, now I know that whenever we do anything for You, You do still more for us. I am going to do so much for You. I am going to try to make others as happy as You have made me."

The Elves and the Shoemaker

Brothers Grimm

There was once a shoemaker, who worked very hard and was very honest: but still he could not earn enough to live upon; and at last all he had in the world was gone, save just leather enough to make one pair of shoes.

Then he cut his leather out, all ready to make up the next day, meaning to rise early in the morning to his work. His conscience was clear and his heart light amidst all his troubles; so he went peaceably to bed, left all his cares to Heaven, and soon fell asleep. In the morning after he had said his prayers, he sat himself down to his work; when, to his great wonder, there stood the shoes already made, upon the table. The good man knew not what to say or think at such an odd thing happening. He looked at the workmanship; there was not one false stitch in the whole job; all was so neat and true, that it was quite a masterpiece.

The same day a customer came in, and the shoes suited him so well that he willingly paid a price higher than usual for them; and the poor shoemaker, with the money, bought leather enough to make two pairs more. In the evening he cut out the work, and went to bed early, that he might get up and begin betimes next day; but he was saved all the trouble, for when he got up in the morning the work was done ready to his hand. Soon in came buyers, who paid him handsomely for his goods, so that he bought leather enough for four pairs more. He cut out the work again overnight and found it done in the morning, as before; and so it went on for some time: what was got ready in the evening was always done by daybreak, and the good man soon became thriving and well off again.

One evening, about Christmas-time, as he and his wife were sitting over the fire chatting together, he said to her, "I should like to sit up and watch tonight, that we may see who it is that comes and does my work for me." The wife liked the thought; so they left a light burning, and hid themselves in a corner of the room, behind a curtain that was hung up there, and watched what would happen.

As soon as it was midnight, there came in two little naked dwarfs; and they sat themselves upon the shoe-maker's bench, took up all the work that was cut out, and began to ply with their little fingers, stitching and rapping and tapping away at such a rate, that the shoemaker was all wonder, and could not take his eyes off them. And on they went, till the job was quite done, and the shoes stood ready for use upon the table. This was long before day-break; and then they bustled away as quick as lightning.

The next day the wife said to the shoemaker, "These little wights have made us rich, and we ought to be thankful to them, and do them a good turn if we can. I am quite sorry to see them run about as they do; and in-deed it is not very decent, for they have nothing upon their backs to keep off the cold. I'll tell you what, I will make each of them a shirt, and a coat and waistcoat, and a pair of pantaloons into the bargain; and do you make each of them a little pair of shoes."

The thought pleased the good cobbler very much; and one evening, when all the things were ready, they laid them on the table, instead of the work that they used to cut out, and then went and hid themselves, to watch what the little elves would do.

About midnight in they came, dancing and skipping, hopped round the room, and then went to sit down to their work as usual; but when they saw the clothes lying for them, they laughed and chuckled, and seemed mightily delighted.

Then they dressed themselves in the twinkling of an eye, and danced and capered and sprang about, as merry as could be; till at last they danced out at the door, and away over the green.

The good couple saw them no more; but everything went well with them from that time forward, as long as they lived.

A Visit from St. Nicholas

Clement C. Moore

'Twas the night before Christmas, when all through the house
Not a creature was stirring, not even a mouse:
The stockings were hung by the chimney with care,
In the hope that St. Nicholas soon would be there.
The children were nestled all snug in their beds,
While visions of sugar-plums danced in their heads;
And Mamma in her kerchief, and I in my cap,
Had just settled our brains for a long winter's nap,
When out on the lawn there rose such a clatter,
I sprang from my bed to see what was the matter.
Away to the window I flew like a flash,
Tore open the shutters, and threw up the sash.
The moon on the breast of the new-fallen snow
Gave the luster of midday to objects below;
When, what to my wondering eyes should appear
But a miniature sleigh, and eight tiny reindeer,
With a little old driver, so lively and quick,
I knew in a moment it must be St. Nick!
More rapid than eagles his coursers they came,
And he whistled, and shouted and called them by name:
"Now, Dasher! now, Dancer! now, Prancer! now, Vixen!
On, Comet! on, Cupid! on, Donder and Blitzen!
To the top of the porch, to the top of the wall,
Now, dash away! dash away! dash away, all!"
As dry leaves, that before the wild hurricane fly
When they meet with an obstacle, mount to the sky,
So, up to the house-top the coursers they flew,
With the sleigh full of toys, and St. Nicholas, too;

And then, in a twinkling, I heard on the roof
The prancing and pawing of each little hoof.
As I drew in my head, and was turning around,
Down the chimney St. Nicholas came with a bound.
He was dressed all in fur from his head to his foot,
And his clothes were all tarnished with ashes and soot;
A bundle of toys he had flung on his back,
And he looked like a peddler just opening his pack;
His eyes, how they twinkled! his dimples, how merry!
His cheeks were like roses, his nose like a cherry;
His droll little mouth was drawn up like a bow,
And the beard on his chin was as white as the snow;
The stump of a pipe he held tight in his teeth,
And the smoke it encircled his head like a wreath;
He had a broad face, and a little round belly,
That shook, when he laughed, like a bowlful of jelly.
He was chubby and plump,-a right jolly old elf-
And I laughed when I saw him, in spite of myself.
A wink of his eye and a twist of his head
Soon gave me to know I had nothing to dread.
He spoke not a word, but went straight to his work,
And filled all the stockings; then turned with a jerk,
And, laying his finger aside of his nose,
And giving a nod, up the chimney he rose.
He sprang to his sleigh, to his team gave a whistle,
And away they all flew like the down of a thistle;
But I heard him exclaim, ere he drove out of sight,
"Merry Christmas to all, and to all a good-night!"

The First
Christmas Tree

Once upon a time the Forest was in a great commotion. Early in the evening the wise old Cedars had shaken their heads and told of strange things that were to happen. They had lived in the Forest many, many years; but never had they seen such marvelous sights as were to be seen now in the sky, and upon the hills, and in the distant village.

"Pray tell us what you see," pleaded a little Vine; "we who are not so tall as you can behold none of these wonderful things."

"The whole sky seems to be aflame," said one of the Cedars, "and the Stars appear to be dancing among the clouds. Angels walk down from heaven to the earth and talk with the shepherds upon the hills."

The Vine trembled with excitement. Its nearest neighbor was a tiny tree, so small it was scarcely ever noticed; yet it was a very beautiful little tree, and the Vines and Ferns and Mosses loved it very dearly.

"How I should like to see the Angels!" sighed the little Tree; "and how I should like to see the Stars dancing among the clouds! It must be very beautiful. Oh, listen to the music! I wonder whence it comes."

"The Angels are singing," said a Cedar; "for none but

Angels could make such sweet music."

"And the Stars are singing, too," said another Cedar; "Yes, and the shepherds on the hills join in the song."

The trees listened to the singing. It was a strange song about a Child that had been born. But further than this they did not understand. The strange and glorious song continued all the night.

In the early morning the Angels came to the Forest singing the same song about the Child, and the Stars sang in chorus with them, until every part of the woods rang with echoes of that wondrous song. They were clad all in white, and there were crowns upon their fair heads, and golden harps in their hands. Love, hope, joy and compassion beamed from their beautiful faces. The Angels came through the Forest to where the little Tree stood, and gathering around it, they touched it with their hands, kissed its little branches, and sang even more sweetly than before. And their song was about the Child, the Child, the Child, that had been born. Then the Stars came down from the skies and danced and hung upon the branches of the little Tree, and they, too, sang the song of the Child.

When they left the Forest, one Angel remained to guard the little Tree. Night and day he watched so that no harm should come to it. Day by day it grew in strength and beauty. The sun sent it his choicest rays, heaven dropped its sweetest dew upon it, and the winds sang to it their prettiest songs.

So the years passed, and the little Tree grew until it became the pride and glory of the Forest.

One day the Tree heard someone coming through the Forest. "Have no fear," said the Angel, "for He who comes is the Master."

And the Master came to the Tree and placed His Hands upon its smooth trunk and branches. He stooped and kissed the Tree, and then turned and went away.

Many times after that the Master came to the Forest, rested beneath the Tree and enjoyed the shade of its foliage. Many times He slept there and the Tree watched over Him. Many times men came with the Master to the Forest, sat with Him in the shade of the Tree, and talked with Him of things which the Tree never could understand. It heard them tell how the Master healed the sick and raised the dead and bestowed blessings wherever He walked.

But one night the Master came alone into the Forest. His Face was pale and wet with tears. He fell upon His knees and prayed. The Tree heard Him, and all the Forest was still. In the morning there was a sound of rude voices and a clashing of swords.

Strange men plied their axes with cruel vigor, and the Tree was hewn to the ground. Its beautiful branches were cut away, and its soft, thick foliage was strewn to the winds. The Trees of the Forest wept.

The cruel men dragged the hewn Tree away, and the Forest saw it no more.

But the Night Wind that swept down from the City of the Great King stayed that night in the Forest awhile to say that it had seen that day a Cross raised on Calvary...the Tree on which was nailed the Body of the dying Master.

Gloria in Excelsis

Gloria in excelsis!
Sound the thrilling song;
In excelsis Deo!
Roll the hymn along.

———— ❋ ————

Gloria in excelsis!
Let the heavens ring;
In excelsis Deo!
Welcome, new-born King.

———— ❋ ————

Gloria in excelsis!
Over the sea and land,
In excelsis Deo!
Chant the anthem grand.

Gloria in excelsis!
Let us all rejoice;
In excelsis Deo!
Lift each heart and voice.

Gloria in excelsis!
Swell the hymn on high;
In excelsis Deo!
Sound it to the sky.

Gloria in excelsis!
Sing it, sinful earth,
In excelsis Deo!
For the Savior's birth.

The Noel Candle

Clement C. Moore

It was Christmas Eve in Rheims, nearly five hundred years ago. The great cathedral towered high above the city, its spires seem to reach to the very skies, and the square in front of the church was thronged with people, celebrating the joyous Noel, the Christmas time. Children darted here and there through the crowd, shrieking with laughter. On one corner a group of well-dressed youths and maidens were dancing to the music of a lute and tambourine; on another a number of boys sang old carols. Others strolled about in groups of two and three, chatting and laughing, while the older and more serious went their way, candle in hand, toward the cathedral, where Masses were being chanted in Latin. Though these church-goers were more quiet, it was evident that they were happy, for their faces shone with contentment. It did not seem that there could be, in all the city of Rheims, one sad or lonely heart.

Yet there were four. Three of them dwelt in a squalid hovel by the riverside, a tiny shed or lean-to which stood beside a stable. Though its outward appearance was so dismal, once within the door, one might have been surprised to see how neat and trim it was kept. There was but one room which served at once as living room, dining room, bed room and kitchen for three people. The rough stone floor was carefully swept and polished. In one corner lay a straw-filled mattress, but the covers drawn over it, though patched and darned in a dozen places, were spotlessly clean. A rude table, a broken chair, a stool and a clumsy bench completed the furniture of the room. In a far corner stood a small charcoal brazier, whose feeble fire served not only to cook the meals, but to warm the dwellers in the hut. Some cracked earthen kettles hung beside it.

There was one touch of brightness and beauty in the little room that was supplied by a tiny shrine, built on a shelf at the rear wall. A few field flowers in a bowl stood before it, and from the edge of the shelf hung a silken sash which once had held a knight's shield. It was of scarlet, heavily embroidered in gold, and bore a devise of a lion, surmounted by the lily of France.

Three people were in the room. A young woman was bending over a small spinning wheel, a boy of seven was setting the table with their few cracked dishes, and a girl a year or so older was leaning over a kettle on the brazier, stirring its contents from time to time. The lady, whose beauty seemed to shine in the poor room, despite her shabby clothing, was Madame la Comtesse Marie de Malincourt, and the boy and girl, her son and daughter, Louis and Jeanne.

As she worked the lady was thinking sadly of that Christmas Eve only a year before, when all had been so different. Then she had lived in a great castle, and on the eve of Noel, as she had done for a half dozen years before, she and her husband and children had gone down to the castle gate to greet the crowd that had assembled. The old, the ailing, and the poor had gathered there, and that meant nearly all the village. Out among the crowd they had gone, followed by a dozen servants, laden down like beasts of burden and to each villager the lady had made gifts of warm clothing, of healing herbs, and of wholesome food. Even Louis and Jeanne, young as they were, had given from their store of toys and baubles to the children of the village.

Then the tide of war had swept over their happy valley; the castle had been attacked, defended, and lost, then sacked by the victors. Lady Marie had even seen them lead her husband away a prisoner. She had fled with her children, down a secret passage out into the night and away to the village. She found it deserted, the villagers driven out before the sword.

During the months that had ensued the three had been wanderers along the highway. Bit by bit Lady Marie had given her jewels and trinkets, then those of the children, in exchange for food and lodging. Even her velvet robe, with its soft fur mantle, had gone to the wife of a rich burgher, and the pretty clothing of Louis and Jeanne had long since been replaced with coarse peasant garb.

One thing alone remained of all their riches – the cover of her husband's shield, which little Louis had brought from the castle that dreadful night. "Father gave it to me to keep until he came back," he said, and through all the terrors of flight he had clung to it. It was very dear to them all. It seemed a bit of their old life, and a constant reminder of the dear lost father.

"Mother," said Jeanne suddenly, interrupting the current of her mother's sad thoughts, "it is Noel tonight."

"Yes, my child," Lady Marie answered with a sigh, "but there will be no toys, or sweets, or pretty things for thee or little Louis this Noel."

"We want them not," the children answered, almost in unison. "We have thee, dear mother, and we can keep the Noel in our hearts," added Jeanne.

Her mother looked up from the wheel and smiled at her. "Yes, though life is hard," she said, "still, we have each other, and though we are sad, perhaps there are other hearts in Rheims that grieve tonight. I wish I might give, as once I did, to the poor, but I have nothing to give. We have ourselves become the poor." She resumed her work, and there was silence in the room save for the whir of the wheel.

"Mother," Jeanne spoke again excitedly, "I know something we can give." As she talked she caught up the small tallow dip candle from the table and hurried with it to the one window of the hut.

"See," she went on, "I will put it here – on the sill – so – and perhaps someone who passes, someone like ourselves lonely and forlorn, will be the happier for my little gift of light. There – see how it shines out on the snow," and she stood back to survey her work.

"You are a good child, Jeanne," said Lady Marie, then, sighing, she resumed her work, her silence, her sad thoughts.

Down in the great square, among all the lights and gaiety, was another sad heart. It beat in the breast of a little lad of nine, a boy whose clothes were shabby and ragged, whose bare feet were thrust into clumsy wooden sabots, and with no covering on his head but his own fair hair. He was utterly alone, without money, without friends, cold, hungry, miserable. When it seemed he could bear this burden alone no longer, he tried to tell his story to some of the smiling people he saw about him. Surely among so many he would find friends. But no one took any interest in him, other than to frown at him, or elbow him roughly out of the way, and one man shook him by the shoulder, and called him a beggar.

He left the square at last in utter discouragement, and began to tramp the streets, stopping now and then at splendid dwellings through whose windows streamed bright lights like a welcoming smile. But there was no welcome for the lonely child. Fat, well-dressed servants turned him away with angry words, and threatened him with their dogs.

It was dark in the streets of Rheims now, and the air was growing colder, but the child tramped on, trying desperately to find shelter before the night closed in. At last, far off down by the river, he saw a tiny gleam of light appear suddenly at a window and he hurried toward it. As he neared it, the boy saw that it was only a small tallow dip at the window of a hovel, the poorest and meanest hut in all Rheims, but the steady light of the tiny flame brought a sudden glow to his heart and he ran forward and knocked at the door.

It was opened in an instant by a little girl, and at once the other two in the room had risen to greet him. In another moment he found himself seated on a stool beside the charcoal brazier. The little girl was rubbing one of his cold hands in her two warm palms, while her brother was holding the other, and a beautiful woman, kneeling at his feet, drew off the wooden shoes, and chafed his icy feet. When he was thoroughly warmed, the little girl dished up into three bowls and a cracked cup the stew which had been simmering on the fire. There was only a little of it, a scant meal for themselves, but she passed the fullest bowl to the stranger and made room for him beside her on the bench.

After a word of blessing, they ate their stew, and never had the thin soup tasted so rich or satisfying to the countess and her children. As they finished, a sudden glowing light filled the room, greater than the brightness of a thousand candles. There was a sound of angel voices, and the stranger child had grown so radiant that they could scarcely bear to look at him.

"Thou, with thy little candle, has lighted the Christ-child on His way to Heaven," said their unknown Guest, His hand on the door latch. "This night shall thy dearest wish be granted thee," and in another instant He was gone.

The countess and her children fell on their knees and prayed, and there they still were, almost a quarter of an hour later, when a knight in shining armour gently pushed open the door and entered the hut.

"Marie! Louis! Jeanne!" he cried in a voice of love and longing. "Do ye not know me after all these weary months of prison and battle, and then of search for thee?"

Immediately his family were clustered about him, and their kisses and embraces were his answer.

"But, Father, how did you find us here," cried little Louis at last, when the first raptures of welcome were over.

"A ragged lad I met on the highway told me ye dwelt here," answered the knight.

"The Christ-Child," said Lady Marie reverently, and told him the story.

And so, forever after, they and all their descendants, have burned a candle in the window on the Eve of Noel, to light the lonely Christ-Child on His way.

A Christmas Legend

Florence Scannell

It was Christmas Eve. The night was very dark and the snow falling fast, as Hermann, the charcoal-burner, drew his cloak tighter around him, and the wind whistled fiercely through the trees of the Black Forest. He had been to carry a load to a castle near, and was now hastening home to his little hut. Although he worked very hard, he was poor, gaining barely enough for the wants of his wife and his four little children. He was thinking of them, when he heard a faint wailing. Guided by the sound, he groped about and found a little child, scantily clothed, shivering and sobbing by itself in the snow.

"Why, little one, have they left thee here all alone to face this cruel blast?"

The child answered nothing, but looked piteously up in the charcoal-burner's face.

"Well, I cannot leave thee here. Thou would'st be dead before the morning."

So saying, Hermann raised it in his arms, wrapping it in his cloak and warming its little cold hands in his bosom. When he arrived at his hut, he put down the child and tapped at the door, which was immediately thrown open, and the children rushed to meet him.

"Here, wife, is a guest to our Christmas Eve supper," said he, leading in the little one, who held timidly to his finger with its tiny hand.

"And welcome he is," said the wife. "Now let him

come and warm himself by the fire."

The children all pressed round to welcome and gaze at the little new-comer. They showed him their pretty fir-tree, decorated with bright, colored lamps in honor of Christmas Eve, which the good mother had endeavored to make a fête for the children.

Then they sat down to supper, each child contributing of its portion for the guest, looking with admiration at its clear, blue eyes and golden hair, which shone so as to shed a brighter light in the little room; and as they gazed, it grew into a sort of halo round his head, and his eyes beamed with a heavenly luster. Soon two white wings appeared at his shoulders, and he seemed to grow larger and larger, and then the beautiful vision vanished, spreading out his hands as in benediction over them.

Hermann and his wife fell on their knees, exclaiming, in awe-struck voices: "The holy Christ-Child!" and then embraced their wondering children in joy and thankfulness that they had entertained the Heavenly Guest.

The next morning, as Hermann passed by the place where he had found the fair child, he saw a cluster of lovely white flowers, with dark green leaves, looking as though the snow itself had blossomed. Hermann plucked some, and carried them reverently home to his wife and children, who treasured the fair blossoms and tended them carefully in remembrance of that wonderful Christmas Eve, calling them Chrysanthemums; and every year, as the time came round, they put aside a portion of their feast and gave it to some poor little child, according to the words of the Christ: "Inasmuch as ye have done it unto one of the least of these My brethren, ye have done it unto Me."

Little Fred Wolff

Once upon a time - so long ago that everybody has forgotten the date - in a city in the north of Europe - with such a hard name that nobody can ever remember it - there was a little seven-year-old boy named Fred Wolff, whose parents were dead, who lived with a cross and stingy old aunt, who never thought of kissing him more than once a year and who sighed deeply whenever she gave him a bowlful of soup.

But the poor little fellow had such a sweet nature that in spite of everything, he loved the old woman, although he was terribly afraid of her and could never look at her ugly old face without shivering.

As this aunt of little Fred was known to have a house of her own and an old woollen stocking full of gold, she had not dared to send the boy to a charity school; but, in order to get a reduction in the price, she had so wrangled with the master of the school, to which little Fred finally went, that this bad man, vexed at having a pupil so poorly dressed and paying so little, often punished him unjustly, and even prejudiced his companions against him, so that the boys, all sons of rich parents, made a drudge and laughing stock of the little fellow. The poor little one was thus as wretched as a child could be and used to hide himself in corners to weep whenever Christmas time came.

It was the schoolmaster's custom to take all his pupils to the Midnight Mass on Christmas Eve, and to bring them home again afterward. Now, as the winter this year was very bitter, and as heavy snow had been falling for several days, all the boys came well bundled up in warm clothes, with fur caps pulled over their ears, padded jackets, gloves and knitted mittens, and strong, thick-soled boots. Only little Fred presented himself shivering in the poor clothes he used to wear both weekdays and Sundays and having on his feet only thin socks in heavy wooden shoes.

His naughty companions noticing his sad face and awkward appearance, made many jokes at his expense; but the little fellow was so busy blowing on his fingers, and was suffering so much with chilblains, that he took no notice of them. So the band of youngsters, walking two and two behind the master, started for the church.

It was pleasant in the church which was brilliant with lighted candles; and the boys, excited by the warmth, took advantage of the music of the choir and the organ to chatter among themselves in low tones. They bragged about the fun that was awaiting them at home. The mayor's son had seen, just before starting off, an immense goose ready stuffed and dressed for cooking.

At the alderman's home there was a little pine-tree with branches laden down with oranges, sweets, and toys. And the lawyer's cook had put on her cap with such care as she never thought of taking unless she was expecting something very good!

Then they talked, too, of all that the Christ-Child was going to bring them, of all he was going to put in their shoes which, you might be sure, they would take good care to leave in the chimney place before going to bed; and the eyes of these little urchins, as lively as a cage of mice, were sparkling in advance over the joy they would have when they awoke in the morning and saw the pink bag full of sugar-plums, the little lead soldiers ranged in companies in their boxes, the menageries smelling of varnished wood, and the magnificent jumping-jacks in purple and tinsel.

Alas! Little Fred knew by experience that his old miser of an aunt would send him to bed supperless, but, with childlike faith and certain of having been, all the year, as good and industrious as possible, he hoped that the Christ-Child would not forget him, and so he, too, planned to place his wooden shoes in good time in the fireplace.

Midnight Mass over, the worshippers departed, eager for their fun, and the band of pupils always walking two and two, and following the teacher, left the church.

Now, in the porch and seated on a stone bench set in the niche of a painted arch, a child was sleeping - a child in a white woollen garment, but with his little feet bare, in spite of the cold. He was not a beggar, for his garment was white and new, and near him on the floor was a bundle of carpenter's tools.

In the clear light of the stars, his face, with its closed eyes, shone with an expression of divine sweetness, and his long, curling, blond locks seemed to form a halo about his brow. But his little child's feet, made blue by the cold of this bitter December night, were pitiful to see!

The boys so well clothed for the winter weather passed by quite indifferent to the unknown child; several of them, sons of the notables of the town, however, cast on the vagabond looks in which could be read all the scorn of the rich for the poor, of the well-fed for the hungry.

But little Fred, coming last out of the church, stopped, deeply touched, before the beautiful sleeping child. "Oh, dear!" said the little fellow to himself, "this is frightful! This poor little one has no shoes and stockings in this bad weather - and, what is still worse, he has not even a wooden shoe to leave near him tonight while he sleeps, into which the little Christ-Child can put something good to soothe his misery."

And carried away by his loving heart, Fred drew the wooden shoe from his right foot, laid it down before the sleeping child, and, as best he could, sometimes hopping, sometimes limping with his sock wet by the snow, he went home to his aunt.

"Look at the good-for-nothing!" cried the old woman, full of wrath at the sight of the shoeless boy. "What have you done with your shoe, you little villain?"

Little Fred did not know how to lie, so, although trembling with terror when he saw the rage of the old shrew, he tried to relate his adventure. But the miserly old creature only burst into a frightful fit of laughter. "Aha! So my young gentleman strips himself for the beggars. Aha! My young gentleman breaks his pair of shoes for a bare-foot! Here is something new, forsooth. Very well, since it is this way, I shall put the only shoe that is left into the chimney-place, and I'll answer for it that the Christ-Child will put in something tonight to beat you with in the morning! And you will have only a crust of bread and water tomorrow. And we shall see if the next time, you will be giving your shoes to the first vagabond that hap-pens along."

And the wicked woman having boxed the ears of the poor little fellow, made him climb up into the loft where he had his wretched cubbyhole.

Desolate, the child went to bed in the dark and soon fell asleep, but his pillow was wet with tears.

But behold! the next morning when the old woman, awakened early by the cold, went downstairs - oh, wonder of wonders - she saw the big chimney filled with shining toys, bags of magnificent bonbons, and riches of every sort, and standing out in front of all this treasure, was the right wooden shoe which the boy had given to the little vagabond, yes, and beside it, the one which she had placed in the chimney to hold the bunch of switches.

As little Fred, attracted by the cries of his aunt, stood in an ecstasy of childish delight before the splendid Christmas gifts, shouts of laughter were heard outside. The woman and child ran out to see what all this meant, and behold! all the gossips of the town were standing around the public fountain. What could have happened? Oh, a most ridiculous and extraordinary thing! The children of the richest men in the town, whom their parents had planned to surprise with the most beautiful gifts had found only switches in their shoes!

Then the old woman and the child thinking of all the riches in their chimney were filled with fear. But suddenly they saw the priest appear, his countenance full of astonishment. Just above the bench placed near the door of the church, in the very spot where, the night before, a child in a white garment and with bare feet, in spite of the cold, had rested his lovely head, the priest had found a circlet of gold imbedded in the old stones.

Then, they all crossed themselves devoutly, perceiving that this beautiful sleeping child with the carpenter's tools had been Jesus of Nazareth Himself, Who had come back for one hour just as He had been when He used to work in the home of His parents; and reverently they bowed before this miracle, which the good God had done to reward the faith and the love of a little child.

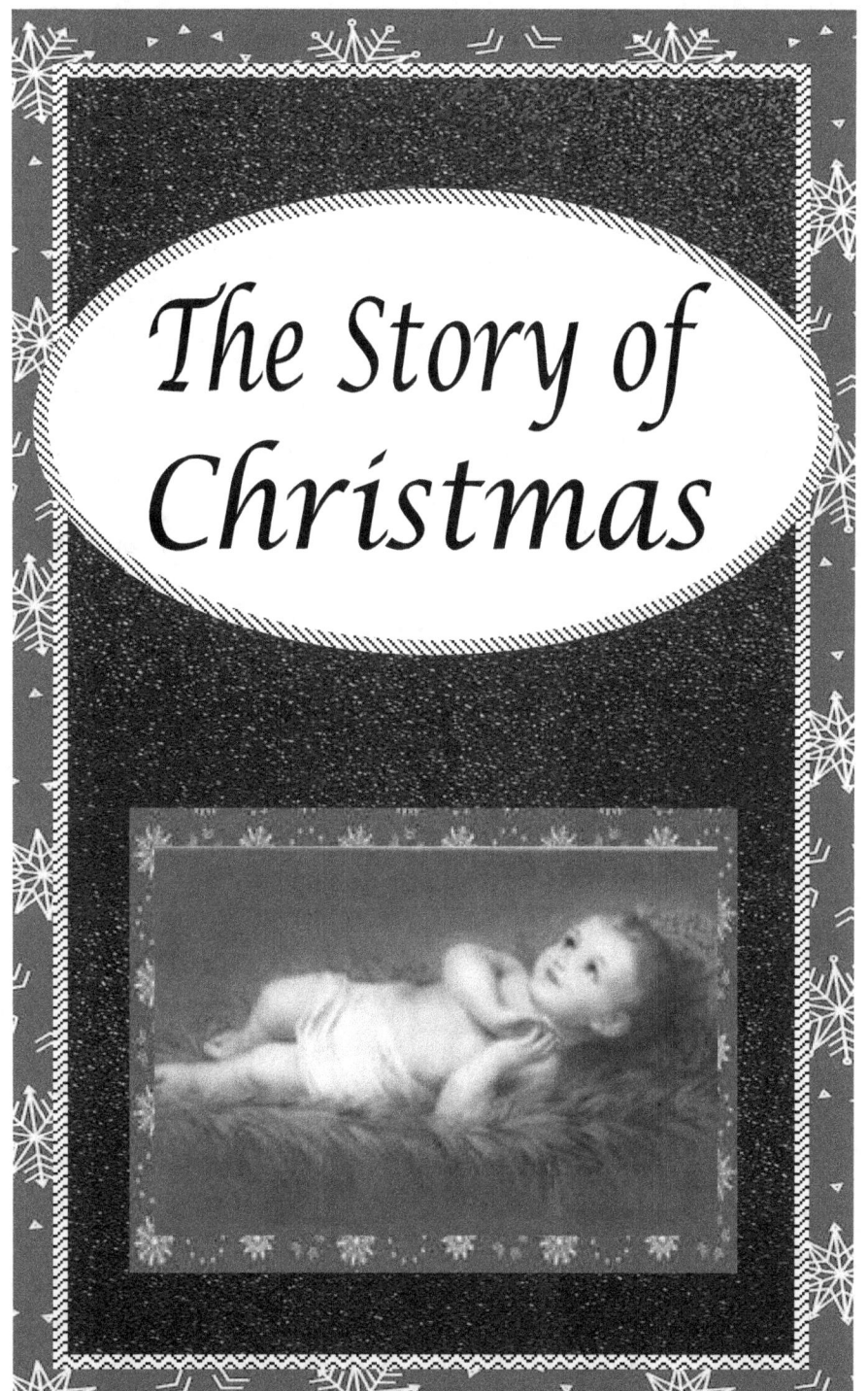

The Story of Christmas

When the time had come in which the Son of God was to become man for love of us, His mother Mary and St. Joseph had to leave their home in Nazareth and go to Bethlehem.

The reason for this journey was that the Roman Emperor wanted to count the number of his subjects, and so every Jewish family had to go to the city of their ancestors. Since Mary and Joseph belonged to the royal family of David, they had to go to David's city of Bethlehem. The Emperor had made the law, but it served to fulfill God's plan, for in the Holy Bible it was written that the Saviour was to be born in Bethlehem.

It was a slow, hard journey for Our Blessed Mother over the mountainous country to Bethlehem, but she knew that she was doing God's Will and she was happy thinking of her Divine Son soon to be born. When Mary and Joseph reached Bethlehem, they found that there was no place for them to stay. At last, they had to go into a cave, where the breath of an ox and a donkey kept them warm.

There in that rough stable, the Son of God was born on Christmas Day. His Blessed Mother wrapped Him in swaddling clothes and laid Him in a manger. Our Lord chose to be born in such poverty so that we would learn not to desire riches and comforts.

The very night in which Jesus was born, God sent His angels to announce His birth. The angels were not sent to the Emperor or the King, or even to the learned doctors and chief priests. They were sent to poor, humble shepherds who were watching their flocks on the hillside near Bethlehem. As soon as they heard the angels' message, the good, simple men hurried to adore the Saviour of the world. Then they went home giving glory to God. The great Patriarchs and Prophets of the Old Testament had been comforted by the thought that someday the Saviour would come into the world. Now that He had come, all good men rejoiced. Christ came for all of us. The Bible says, "God so loved the world that He sent His only-begotten Son." If those who lived in the hope of His coming were happy, how much more ought we to rejoice!

We have His teachings, His Church, and even Jesus Himself. Christmas is the time when we realize more than ever how much God loves us!

Jesus' Birthday

How happy you are every year, my little children, as Christmas Day draws nearer and nearer! But do you know that long ago there was no such thing as Christmas Day? However, people knew that sometime one would come, for they had been told ages and ages ago, when Adam and Eve sinned and the gates of Heaven had been closed, had they not been told, I say, that God would send His Son who would show the people how to be good and happy again, and reopen the gates of Paradise?

The time was now drawing near when the promise was to be carried out. The King of heaven and earth was to come into this world quietly. Who was the first to know it, dear children? The loveliest creature that ever lived, the modest maid of Galilee in whose sweet face shone goodness and purity. This beautiful maiden was called Mary. She is no other than our own dear Blessed Mother. Mary lived in the peaceful little village of Nazareth. Her home was the poor cottage of St. Joseph, the village carpenter.

One day as Mary was at prayer, suddenly a soft light filled the room and the angel Gabriel appeared, saying: "Hail, full of grace, the Lord is with thee; blessed art thou among women." As Mary gazed in wonder at the beautiful angel, he went on to tell her that she was to be the Mother of a Child 'Whom she should call Jesus.' Later, the same angel appeared to St. Joseph, telling him that he was to be the foster-father of Jesus.

Time went on, and an emperor of Rome wished to

know just how many people he ruled over, so he sent out word that every man should go to the city where his family belonged and write his name in a large book.

Now, not very far from Jerusalem there was a little town called Bethlehem, the city of David, and St. Joseph and the Virgin Mary had to go to have their names taken down, for both belonged to the family of David.

Of course there were many, many others who had to go there, too, and Bethlehem, being only a very small place, every house was soon filled. It was quite late when St. Joseph and Mary arrived and nowhere could they find a room for the night; but at last someone told them of a cave close by which was used for a stable, and even then there were some animals in it.

But St. Joseph and Blessed Mary were so tired from the long journey that they were glad to find a place to rest, even if it were a rough stable open to the cold winds. Here at midnight the Infant Jesus was born in cold and poverty; he did not even have a bed to lie in, and His Blessed Mother wrapped Him in swaddling clothes and laid Him in a manger, the only cradle she had for her dear Baby.

So, the little town of Bethlehem slept through the first Christmas night, and did not know that its Saviour had been born. Such, children, is the sweet story of Bethlehem and the Infant Jesus.

Good King Wenceslaus

One of the most popular Christmas carols ever written was *Good King Wenceslaus*. The story of the saint about whom it is written is almost as much fun to learn about as the carol is to sing.

Wenceslaus was not a king, although he was very good. The man who wrote the song, John Mason Neale, knew that Wenceslaus was actually the duke of Bohemia, but he must have felt that 'king' was the best way to describe him. Bohemia was an independent state and is now in Czechoslovakia. The traditional ruler was a duke.

Because she was to become a saint, the story of Saint Wenceslaus actually begins with his grandmother, Saint Ludmilla.

Ludmilla and her husband, Borivoi, who was the duke of Bohemia, learned of Christ's love and His message of peace around the year 874 AD. They were baptized into the Christian faith. Although Saint Methodius baptized not only the rulers, but also many of the people of their court, some of the great Bohemian nobles kept for themselves a cruel and harsh pagan religion and were suspicious of the new Christians.

Borivoi and Ludmilla had a son whom they named Wratislaw, and raised him as a Christian. When he grew up, he married a woman named Drahomira. Together, they had a son whom they named Wenceslaus, who would one day become the duke of Bohemia after his father died. Because Ludmilla did not think that Drahomira was a true Christian at heart, she brought up her grandson herself, and taught him about the Christian religion, with the help of her chaplain. Wenceslaus grew in love of God, prayer and virtue, and was a very good student. Some people say that he could even speak Latin as well as a bishop!

Wratislaw was killed in battle before Wenceslaus was old enough to become duke, and Drahomira seized control of the government. Ludmilla realized that she had been right – Drahomira had never been a sincere Christian, and had come up with a policy directed against Bohemia's Christians.

Ludmilla, who was horrified to see all the work of herself and her husband undone, advised Wenceslaus to take control of the government from his mother. Then Ludmilla fled to her castle at Tetin, hoping to spend the rest of her days in prayer and penance. However, Draho- mira firmly believed that Wenceslaus could not take the government from her without his grandmother's help, so she sent two of her supporters to Tetin, and they murdered Ludmilla.

But Drahomira's evil plot failed, and the Christian supporters of Wenceslaus and Ludmilla drove her into exile. As a result, Wenceslaus became the first Christian duke of Bohemia, but his grandmother did not live to see it. As duke, Wenceslaus' first act was to pardon his mother, and allow her to come back to the court. Since he was a Christian, he based his political rule on the Christian faith. His people loved him for his generosity, his concern for justice, and for the sternness with which he punished his nobles who had oppressed the poor. His psalter was worn from very common usage, and he spent many long hours in prayer.

But the good duke Wenceslaus lived in uncivilized times. Not all of his subjects respected him. Some of his nobles thought that Wenceslaus should have been a bishop. They were absolutely horrified when they discovered that he was signing a treaty with the Germans, enemies of the Bohemians. This holy ruler's action was a signal to his enemies to try to end his life and his reign. His enemies were led by Drahomira and his younger brother, Boleslav.

While visiting his brother on September 27, 935, Wenceslaus went to church to celebrate the feasts of Saints Cosmos and Damian. Although legends say that Wenceslaus was told that his life was in danger as soon as the service was finished, he did not pay any attention to those warnings. The next morning, Wenceslaus was on his way to the church, and met his brother. He greeted Boleslav and thanked him for his kindness and hospitality. Boleslav answered him, "Yesterday I tried to serve you as fittingly as I could, but I must serve you with this today," and saying thus, he tried to stab Wenceslaus with his sword.

As the brothers fought, other pagan nobles stabbed Wenceslaus. As he was dying, Wenceslaus whispered, "May God forgive you for this, Boleslav."

People in many places have always remembered Wenceslaus. It has been said that he 'kept the faith, fed the hungry, clothed the naked and cared for everyone'.

When John Mason Neale started writing a Christmas carol for Saint Stephen's feast day, his ideas went straight to Wenceslaus. He created a new legend in his song in order to keep this holy ruler's example fresh in the minds and hearts of the young people today.

Saint Ludmilla's feast is celebrated on September 16 in many countries. Saint Wenceslaus is remembered on Saint Stephen's day, December 26, as well as every time we sing *Good King Wenceslaus*.

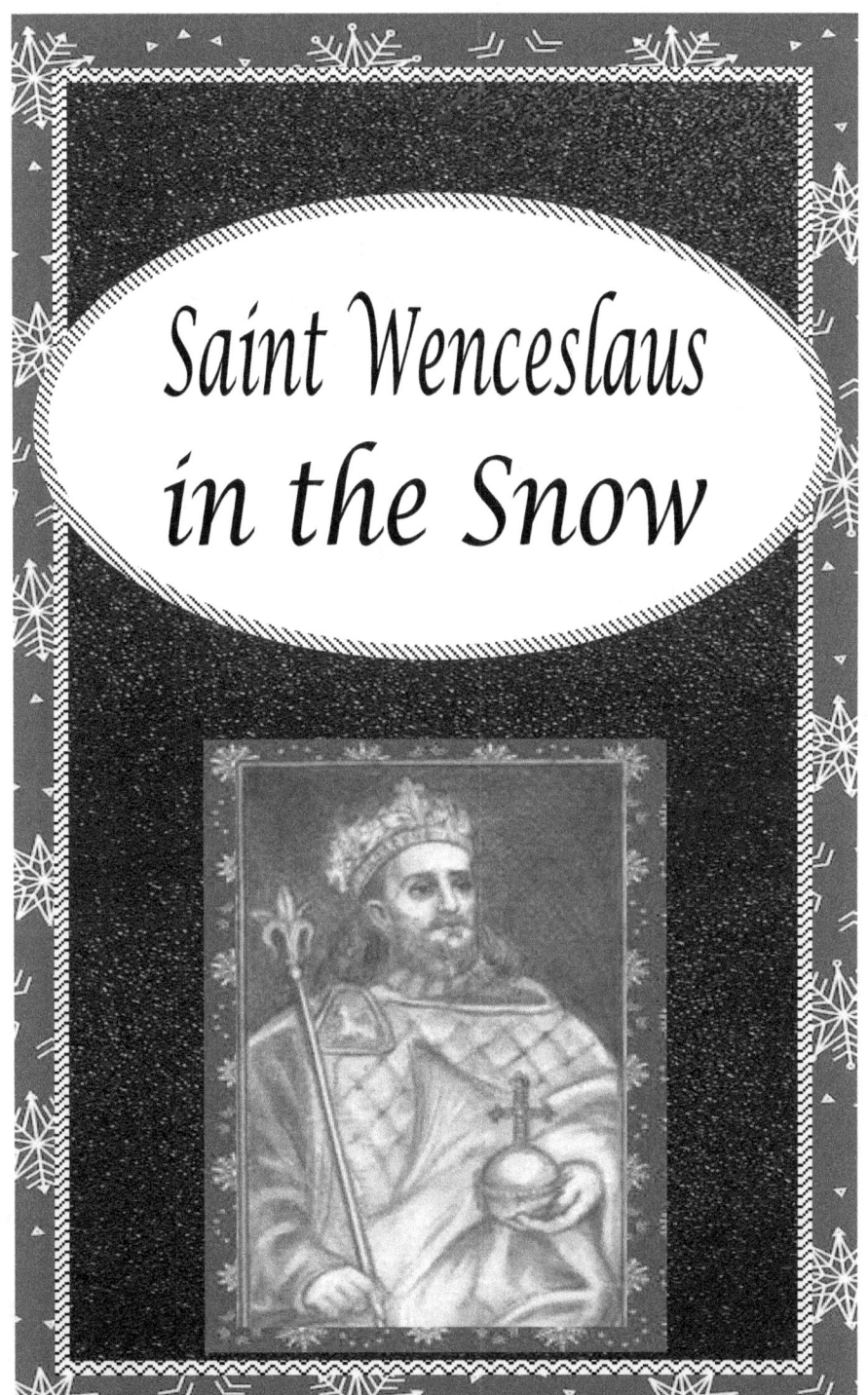

Saint Wenceslaus in the Snow

Imitation is the sincerest flattery and the best way to honour the saints and through them to honour God is to follow their example.

On one very severe and snowy night St. Wenceslaus was on his way to make a visit to the Blessed Sacrament in the neighbouring church. His servant who accompanied him complained that his feet, though well shod, were numb with cold, while the saint, who wore but sandals, seemed not to suffer at all. "Put your feet into the prints of mine, and fear not," said the saint. This the servant did, and presently a genial warmth spread from his feet throughout his whole body.

This is a lively example of what takes place in the soul of the Christian who tries to walk in the footsteps of the saints by imitating their virtues.

The Star

Florence M. Kingsley

Once upon a time in a country far away from here, there lived a little girl named Ruth. Ruth's home was not at all like our houses, for she lived in a little tower on top of the great stone wall that surrounded the town of Bethlehem. Ruth's father was the hotel-keeper--the Bible says the "inn keeper." This inn was not at all like our hotels, either. There was a great open yard, which was called the courtyard. All about this yard were little rooms and each traveler who came to the hotel rented one.

The inn stood near the great stone wall of the city, so that as Ruth stood, one night, looking out of the tower window, she looked directly into the courtyard. It was truly a strange sight that met her eyes. So many people were coming to the inn, for the King had made a law that every man should come back to the city where his father used to live to be counted and to pay his taxes. Some of the people came on the backs of camels, with great rolls of bedding and their dishes for cooking upon the back of the beast. Some of them came on little donkeys, and on their backs too were the bedding and the dishes. Some of the people came walking--slowly; they were so tired. Many miles some of them had come.

As Ruth looked down into the courtyard, she saw the camels being led to their places by their masters, she heard the snap of the whips, she saw the sparks shoot up from the fires that were kindled in the courtyard, where each person was preparing his own supper; she heard the cries of the tired, hungry little children.

Presently her mother, who was cooking supper, came over to the window and said, "Ruthie, thou shalt hide in the house until all those people are gone. Dost thou understand?"

"Yes, my mother," said the child, and she left the window to follow her mother back to the stove, limping painfully, for little Ruth was a cripple. Her mother stooped suddenly and caught the child in her arms.

"My poor little lamb. It was a mule's kick, just six years ago, that hurt your poor back and made you lame."

"Never mind, my mother. My back does not ache today, and lately when the light of the strange new star has shone down upon my bed my back has felt so much stronger and I have felt so happy, as though I could climb upon the rays of the star and up, up into the sky and above the stars!"

Her mother shook her head sadly. "Thou art not likely to climb much, now or ever, but come, the supper is ready; let us go to find your father. I wonder what keeps him."

They found the father standing at the gate of the courtyard, talking to a man and woman who had just arrived. The man was tall, with a long beard, and he led by a rope a snow white mule, on which sat the drooping figure of the woman.

As Ruth and her mother came near, they heard the father say, "But I tell thee that there is no more room in the inn. Hast thou no friends where thou canst go to spend the night?" The man shook his head. "No, none," he answered. "I care not for myself, but my poor wife." Little Ruth pulled at her mother's dress. "Mother, the oxen sleep out under the stars these warm nights and the straw in the caves is clean and warm; I have made a bed there for my little lamb."

Ruth's mother bowed before the tall man. "Thou didst hear the child. It is as she says--the straw is clean and warm." The tall man bowed his head. "We shall be very glad to stay," and he helped the sweet-faced woman down from the donkey's back and led her away to the cave stable, while the little Ruth and her mother hurried up the stairs that they might send a bowl of porridge to the sweet-faced woman, and a sup of new milk, as well.

That night when little Ruth lay down in her bed, the

rays of the beautiful new star shone through the window more brightly than before. They seemed to soothe the tired aching shoulders. She fell asleep and dreamed that the beautiful, bright star burst and out of it came countless angels, who sang in the night:

"Glory to God in the highest, peace on earth, to men of good will." And then it was morning and her mother was bending over her and saying, "Awake, awake, little Ruth. Mother has something to tell thee." Then as the eyes opened slowly-- "The angels came in the night, little one, and left a Baby to lay beside your little white lamb in the manger."

That afternoon, Ruth went with her mother to the fountain. The mother turned aside to talk to the other women of the town about the strange things heard and seen the night before, but Ruth went on and sat down by the edge of the fountain.

The child was not frightened, for strangers came often to the well, but never had she seen men who looked like the three who now came towards her. The first one, a tall man with a long white beard, came close to Ruth and said, "Canst thou tell us, child, where is born He that is called the King of the Jews?"

"I know of no king," she answered, "but last night

while the star was shining, the angels brought a baby to lie beside my white lamb in the manger." The stranger bowed his head. "That must be He. Wilt thou show us the way to Him, my child?" So Ruth ran and her mother led the three men to the cave and 'when they saw the Child, they rejoiced with exceeding great joy, and opening their gifts, they presented unto Him gold, and frankincense and myrrh,' with wonderful jewels, so that Ruth's mother's eyes shone with wonder, but little Ruth saw only the Baby, which lay asleep on its mother's breast.

"If only I might hold Him in my arms," she thought, but was afraid to ask.

After a few days, the strangers left Bethlehem, all but the three--the man, whose name was Joseph, and Mary, his wife, and the Baby. Then, as of old, little Ruth played about the courtyard and the white lamb frolicked at her side. Often she dropped to her knees to press the little woolly white head against her breast, while she murmured: "My little lamb, my very, very own. I love you, lambie," and then together they would steal over to the entrance of the cave to peep in at the Baby, and always she thought, "If I only might touch His hand," but was afraid to ask.

One night as she lay in her bed, she thought to herself: "Oh, I wish I had a beautiful gift for Him, such as the wise men brought, but I have nothing at all to offer and I love Him so much." Just then the light of the star, which was nightly fading, fell across the foot of the bed and shone full upon the white lamb which lay asleep at her feet --and then she thought of something.

The next morning she arose with her face shining with joy. She dressed carefully and with the white lamb held close to her breast, went slowly and painfully down the stairway and over to the door of the cave. "I have come," she said, "to worship Him, and I have brought Him--my white lamb."

The mother smiled at the lame child, then she lifted the Baby from her breast and placed Him in the arms of the little maid who knelt at her feet.

A few days after, an angel came to the father, Joseph, and told him to take the Baby and hurry to the land of Egypt, for the wicked King wanted to do it harm, and so these three--the father, mother and Baby--went by night to the far country of Egypt.

And the star grew dimmer and dimmer and passed away forever from the skies over Bethlehem, but little Ruth grew straight and strong and beautiful as the almond trees in the orchard, and all the people who saw her were amazed, for Ruth was once a cripple.

"It was the light of the strange star," her mother said, but little Ruth knew it was the touch of the blessed Christ-Child, who was once folded against her heart.

Saint Thomas Becket
Archbishop of Canterbury

King Henry II's men had threatened Archbishop Thomas, and he knew he was going to be killed. However, he did not seem disturbed as the procession of monks and clerks slowly wound their way into the dark Cathedral, chanting Vespers. First came the monks, lighting the way with their candles; then came the clerks, slowly, two by two. Finally, the tall Archbishop entered, hurried on by two friends, who immediately ordered the doors to be locked and barred. But Thomas quickly changed the order saying, "Under holy obedience, I command that you open the doors. The House of God should not be turned into a castle." The monks could not, and would not, disobey.

Years before, King Henry II of England had made Thomas Becket the Chancellor of England. Besides the king, this was one of the most powerful positions in the kingdom. As Chancellor, and as Henry's very good friend, Thomas ran the country quite well. He was very popular; he dressed in rich garments and was considered, by Henry II, the most dependable man in England.

Archbishop Theobold of Canterbury died some time later, and Henry told Thomas that he should be his successor. But Thomas knew that Henry wanted to take things from the Church that did not rightfully belong to him, and so Thomas told him that. But Henry would have his way, ignoring Thomas' prophetic statement that "our friendship will turn to hatred". Thomas was ordained a priest on Saturday, June 2, 1162. Then he was consecrated a bishop on Trinity Sunday, which happened to be the very next day. Thomas changed his way of life and started practicing secret penances, fastings, constant prayer and more. This began to annoy Henry, and the friendship between the two became more and more distant.

Henry began to desire that the donations of the people went to him instead of to the Church. He refused to let any bishops leave England without his permission, and he wanted to select his friends as the bishops of England. But the Church would not allow Henry to do any of this, and Thomas opposed him. Then a kind of peace was temporarily made between the Archbishop and the King, but something again sent Henry into a blind rage. In one of his fits of anger he shouted: "Will no one rid me of that Archbishop?" Four of Henry's knights were only too glad to do so. They left the palace shortly after to find the Archbishop Thomas. Henry soon forgot what he had said, but it was too late.

The knights burst into the Cathedral and shouted: "Where is the traitor?" Thomas calmly stepped forward out of the shadows, and replied, "Here I am, no traitor, but a priest of God." The knights tried to drag Thomas from the Cathedral, but couldn't. They finally beat him to death right where he stood.

Thomas' martyrdom greatly affected the people. Within a very short time devotion to him was spread all over Europe. Before two years had passed, King Henry walked barefoot to the tomb and allowed himself to be scourged by the monks. Countless miracles were worked and Thomas Becket, the Archbishop of Canterbury, accomplished in death what he had worked for in life.

The Shepherd Boy

Shamar was a little shepherd boy who lived in Palestine at the time when Our Lord was born as a little Babe at Bethlehem, over two thousand years ago. Poor little Shamar! Why poor? Oh, because he was blind.

One night – it was the first Christmas night – he heard a heavenly voice speaking mysterious words to the shepherds with whom he was camping on the plains near the ancient city of David. There were words about a Child, Christ the King, about tidings of great joy, and then some singing such as he had never heard before – singing, the tender sweetness of which thrilled him through and through. Then there had been some excited talk among the shepherds tenting there and nearly all of them had hastened away. Shamar wondered.

Early in the morning, however, they all returned, and Shamar had to wonder no longer. The other shepherd boys gathered round him and eagerly told him what they had heard and seen. "Angels appeared to us in a glow of light," they said, "and told us of the new-born King – Who is Christ the Lord, the long-expected Messiah. They said we would find him in a stable at Bethlehem, and we hastened thither. And lo, what a lovely sight! There is a poor stable-cave on a hillside. We found the Babe with his foster-father and His Mother. He was lying on the straw in a manger, wrapped in swaddling clothes; and His Mother, the sweetest, dearest Lady in the world, was watching over Him tenderly. His foster-father, Joseph, was kneeling there. An ox and a donkey were in the stable, looking on.

The Babe was so beautiful we could not take our eyes off Him. He was cold, though, and suffering. Still, He looked at us and smiled and stretched out His little hands. He wanted us to come to Him – and oh! His Mother let us kiss Him!"

And all that morning they spoke of nothing but the Babe, the Babe, the Babe. They were going to see Him again that afternoon.

"Oh, do take me with you!" Shamar cried. "I, too, want to visit the little King. Lead me by the hand – please do!"

"But why should you go?" one of the boys, Isaac, asked him. "What will you do there? You are blind, you cannot see." And he would not offer to take him.

Now, Shamar had a little pet lamb with fleece as white as snow and soft as down, which followed and led him around everywhere. He loved that tiny lamb more than anything else in the world; it was the best friend he had on earth. Isaac had often asked for the lamb, but he would never give it to him. Now, however, he wanted to see the Babe at Bethlehem so badly that he said, "Isaac, if you take me along to the stable, to the Babe, I will give you my little lamb." This the boy gladly agreed to; it was a great bargain.

So that afternoon Isaac took Shamar by the hand and led him along to the stable on the hillside. And he took the little lamb, too. He was going to give it away to the new-born King. It would be such a nice present.

They entered the poor, rough cave. With eyes that could not see, Shamar looked towards the place where the Babe lay on the straw. Then from his breast he took his shepherd's flute and began to play his very best pieces for Bethlehem's Boy.

And when Jesus heard the lovely music he looked towards the poor blind shepherd boy and smiled.

The smile was a ray of heavenly sunshine to the lad's darkened eyes. It gave him back his sight and he saw – saw the Child and His Mother and dear St. Joseph, and the ox and the donkey, and everything, just as his comrades had told him.

And kneeling down he adored the Babe Who had restored his sight to reward him for his boyish goodness of heart. And he kissed the little hands stretched out to bless him.

The Little Match Girl

Hans Christian Anderson

Most terribly cold it was; it snowed, and was nearly quite dark, and evening—the last evening of the year. In this cold and darkness there went along the street a poor little girl, bareheaded, and with naked feet. When she left home she had slippers on, it is true; but what was the good of that? They were very large slippers, which her mother had hitherto worn; so large were they; and the poor little thing lost them as she scuffled away across the street, because of two carriages that rolled by dreadfully fast.

One slipper was nowhere to be found; the other had been laid hold of by an urchin, and off he ran with it; he thought it would do capitally for a cradle when he some day or other should have children himself. So the little maiden walked on with her tiny naked feet, that were quite red and blue from cold. She carried a quantity of matches in an old apron, and she held a bundle of them in her hand. Nobody had bought anything of her the whole live-long day; no one had given her a single farthing.

She crept along trembling with cold and hunger--a very picture of sorrow, the poor little thing!

The flakes of snow covered her long fair hair, which fell in beautiful curls around her neck; but of that, of course, she never once now thought. From all the windows the candles were gleaming, and it smelt so deli-ciously of roast goose, for you know it was New Year's Eve; yes, of that she thought.

In a corner formed by two houses, of which one advanced more than the other, she seated herself down and cowered together. Her little feet she had drawn close up to her, but she grew colder and colder, and to go home she did not venture, for she had not sold any matches and could not bring a farthing of money: from her father she would certainly get blows, and at home it was cold, too, for above her she had only the roof, through which the wind whistled, even though the largest cracks were stopped up with straw and rags.

Her little hands were almost numbed with cold. Oh! a match might afford her a world of comfort, if she only dared take a single one out of the bundle, draw it against the wall, and warm her fingers by it. She drew one out. "Rischt!" how it blazed, how it burnt! It was a warm, bright flame, like a candle, as she held her hands over it: it was a wonderful light. It seemed really to the little maiden as though she were sitting before a large iron stove, with burnished brass feet and a brass ornament at top. The fire burned with such blessed influence; it warmed so delightfully. The little girl had already stretched out her feet to warm them too; but--the small flame went out, the stove vanished: she had only the remains of the burnt-out match in her hand.

She rubbed another against the wall: it burned brightly, and where the light fell on the wall, there the wall became transparent like a veil, so that she could see into the room. On the table was spread a snow-white tablecloth; upon it was a splendid porcelain service, and the roast goose was steaming famously with its stuffing of apple and dried plums. And what was still more capital to behold was, the goose hopped down from the dish, reeled about on the floor with knife and fork in its breast, till it came up to the poor little girl; when--the match went out and nothing but the thick, cold, damp wall was left behind. She lighted another match. Now there she was sitting under the most magnificent Christmas tree: it was still larger, and more decorated than the one which she had seen through the glass door in the rich merchant's house.

Thousands of lights were burning on the green branches, and gaily-colored pictures, such as she had seen in the shop-windows, looked down upon her. The little maiden stretched out her hands towards them when--the match went out. The lights of the Christmas tree rose higher and higher, she saw them now as stars in heaven; one fell down and formed a long trail of fire.

"Someone is just dead!" said the little girl; for her old grandmother, the only person who had loved her, and who was now no more, had told her, that when a star falls, a soul ascends to God.

She drew another match against the wall: it was again light, and in the luster there stood the old grandmother, so bright and radiant, so mild, and with such an expression of love.

"Grandmother!" cried the little one. "Oh, take me

with you! You go away when the match burns out; you vanish like the warm stove, like the delicious roast goose, and like the magnificent Christmas tree!" And she rubbed the whole bundle of matches quickly against the wall, for she wanted to be quite sure of keeping her grandmother near her. And the matches gave such a brilliant light that it was brighter than at noon-day: never formerly had the grandmother been so beautiful and so tall. She took the little maiden, on her arm, and both flew in brightness and in joy so high, so very high, and then above was neither cold, nor hunger, nor anxiety--they were with God.

But in the corner, at the cold hour of dawn, sat the poor girl, with rosy cheeks and with a smiling mouth, leaning against the wall--frozen to death on the last evening of the old year. Stiff and stark sat the child there with her matches, of which one bundle had been burnt. "She wanted to warm herself," people said. No one had the slightest suspicion of what beautiful things she had seen; no one even dreamed of the splendor in which, with her grandmother she had entered on the joys of a new year.

The Three Kings of Cologne

Eugene Field

From out of Cologne there came three kings
To worship Jesus Christ, their King.
To Him they sought fine herbs they brought,
And many a beauteous golden thing;
They brought their gifts to Bethlehem town,
And in that manger set them down.

Then spoke the first king, and he said:
"O Child, most heavenly, bright and fair!
I bring this crown to Bethlehem town
For Thee and only Thee, to wear;
So give a heavenly crown to me
When I shall come at last to Thee!"

The second, then. "I bring Thee here
This royal robe, O Child!" he cried;
"Of silk 'tis spun, and such a one
There is not in the world beside;
So in the day of doom requite
Me with a heavenly robe of white!"

The third king gave his gift, and quoth:
"Spikenard and myrrh to Thee I bring,
And with these twain would I most fain
Anoint the body of my King;
So may their incense sometime rise
To plead for me in yonder skies!"

Thus spake the three kings of Cologne,
That gave their gifts, and went their way;
And now kneel I in prayer hard today;
Nor crown, nor robe, nor spice I bring
As offering unto Christ, my King.

Yet have I brought a gift the Child
May not despise, however small;
For here I lay my heart today,
And it is full of love to all.
Take Thou the poor but loyal thing,
My only tribute, Christ, my King!
~*Eugene Field*

The Three Holy Kings

In a far country, in the days before Jesus was born in Judea, there were great astronomers who studied the heavens by night and by day, for they knew of the prophecy which said that a star shall be born or spring out of Jacob, and a man shall arise of the lineage of Israel. And twelve of them were chosen to take heed, who every year ascended upon a mountain which was called the Hill of Victory. Three days they abode there, and prayed our Lord that He would show to them the star that Balaam had said and prophesied.

Now it happened on a time, that they were there on the day of the Nativity of Jesus Christ, and a star came over them upon this mountain, which had the form of a right fair child, and under his head was a shining cross, and from this cross came a voice saying: "To-day is there born a King in Judea."

Now in Arabia, the land in which the soil is red with gold, there reigned a king called Melchior. And in Saba, where frankincense flows from the trees, the king Balthasar ruled. And in the land where myrrh hangs from the bushes, the kingdom of Tharsis, reigned a third king, called Caspar. These three kings also saw the star and heard the voice, and they each made ready to go on a journey. And no one of the three knew that the others intended thus to make a pilgrimage. And they gathered together their treasures to present to the king whom they should seek, and summoned those who should attend them. So each set out with a great company and great estate. And as they journeyed they found the mountains made level as the plains, while the swollen rivers became as dry land. And never did they lose sight of the star, which shined upon them as the sun, always moving before them to guide them on their way.

But when they were come within two miles of Jerusalem, the star disappeared, a heavy fog arose, and each party halted; Melchior, as it fell out, taking his stand on Mount Calvary, Balthasar on the Mount of Olives, and Caspar just between them. And when the fog cleared away, each was astonished to see two other great companies besides his own, and then the kings first discovered that all had come upon the same errand, and they embraced with great joy, and rode together into Jerusalem.

And when they came into the city, Herod and all the people were troubled, because of their so great company like unto an army. Then they demanded in what place the King of the Jews was born, for, said they, "We have seen His star in the Orient, and therefore we come to worship Him." And when Herod had heard this, he was much troubled, and all Jerusalem with him. Then Herod called all the priests of the law, and the doctors, and demanded of them where Jesus Christ should be born. And when he had understood them that He should be born in Bethlehem, he called the three kings apart and demanded of them diligently the time that the star appeared to them. And he said to them that as soon as they should have found the Child and have worshipped

Him, that they should return and show it to him, feigning that he would worship Him also, though he thought that he would go to slay Him.

And as soon as the kings were entered into Jerusalem, the sight of the star was taken from them. But when they were issued out of the city, the star appeared again and went before them, until it came above the place in Bethlehem where the Child was. And they had journeyed now full thirteen days.

And when they had entered into the place they worshipped the young Child. Now the kings had brought great treasures with them, for it must be known that all that Alexander the Great left at his death, and all that the Queen of Sheba gave to King Solomon, and all that Solomon collected for the temple, had descended to the three kings from their ancestors; and all this they had now brought with them. But when they had bowed down before the Child, they were filled with fear and amazement because of the so great light which was in the place. And they each offered quickly the first thing that came to their hands, and forgot all their other gifts. Melchior offered thirty golden pennies, Balthasar gave frankincense, and Caspar myrrh; but all else they quite forgot, and only remembered that they bowed before the Child, and said "Thanks be to God."

And when they would have stayed to do honor to the Holy Child, an angel came to them in a dream, to warn them against Herod, who would do them harm. So they departed each to his own country, journeying for two years. And they preached unto the people, telling them of the new-born King, and everywhere upon the temples men placed the figures of a star, the Child, and a cross.

Now it happened years later that St. Thomas the Apostle journeyed to the far country to preach, and that he wondered why the star was placed upon the temples. Then the priests in those temples told him about the three kings and how they had journeyed to Bethlehem and had seen the young Child.

And the three kings were very old and feeble, but when they heard about St. Thomas, each set out from his own place to go to meet him. And when they had come together they built them a city, and lived together there for two years, worshipping God and preaching. Then Melchior died, and was buried in a large and costly tomb. And when Balthasar died, he, too, was buried there. And at last Caspar was placed beside his companions.

Now in the days of Constantine the Great, his mother Helena determined to find the bodies of the three kings, and for this she made a journey to the far country. And when she had found them, she brought them to Constantinople to the Church of St. Sophia, where they were held in much honor. And from Constantinople they were taken to Milan, where again many pilgrims came. Now when Frederick Barbarossa laid siege to the city of

Milan, he rejoiced above all else to find them there. And by him they were taken to Cologne, and there a golden shrine was built in which the bones of the three holy kings were placed that there they might remain until the Judgment Day.

The Three Kings

Henry Wadsworth Longfellow

Three Kings came riding from far away,
Melchior and Gaspar and Balthasar;
Three Wise Men out of the East were they,
And they travelled by night and they slept by day,
For their guide was a beautiful, wonderful star.
The star was so beautiful, large and clear,
That all the other stars of the sky
Became a white mist in the atmosphere,
And by this they knew that the coming was near
Of the Prince foretold in the prophecy.
Three caskets they bore on their saddle-bows,
Three caskets of gold with golden keys;
Their robes were of crimson silk with rows
Of bells and pomegranates and furbelows,
Their turbans like blossoming almond-trees.
And so the Three Kings rode into the West,
Through the dusk of the night, over hill and dell,
And sometimes they nodded with beard on breast,
And sometimes talked, as they paused to rest,
With the people they met at some wayside well.
"Of the child that is born," said Balthasar,
"Good people, I pray you, tell us the news;
For we in the East have seen his star,
And have ridden fast, and have ridden far,
To find and worship the King of the Jews."
And the people answered, "You ask in vain;
We know of no King but Herod the Great!"
They thought the Wise Men were men insane,
As they spurred their horses across the plain,
Like riders in haste, who cannot wait.
And when they came to Jerusalem,
Herod the Great, who had heard this thing,

Sent for the Wise Men and questioned them;
And said, "Go down unto Bethlehem,
And bring me tidings of this new king."
So they rode away; and the star stood still,
The only one in the grey of morn;
Yes, it stopped —it stood still of its own free will,
Right over Bethlehem on the hill,
The city of David, where Christ was born.
And the Three Kings rode through the gate and the
guard,
Through the silent street, till their horses turned
And neighed as they entered the great inn-yard;
But the windows were closed, and the doors were
barred,
And only a light in the stable burned.
And cradled there in the scented hay,
In the air made sweet by the breath of kine,
The little child in the manger lay,
The child, that would be king one day
Of a kingdom not human, but divine.
His mother Mary of Nazareth
Sat watching beside his place of rest,
Watching the even flow of his breath,
For the joy of life and the terror of death
Were mingled together in her breast.
They laid their offerings at his feet:
The gold was their tribute to a King,
The frankincense, with its odor sweet,
Was for the Priest, the Paraclete,
The myrrh for the body's burying.
And the mother wondered and bowed her head,
And sat as still as a statue of stone;

Her heart was troubled yet comforted,
Remembering what the Angel had said
Of an endless reign and of David's throne.
Then the Kings rode out of the city gate,
With a clatter of hoofs in proud array;
But they went not back to Herod the Great,
For they knew his malice and feared his hate,
And returned to their homes by another way.

Christmas Poems

Christmas is Coming

Christmas is coming,
The geese are getting fat,
Please put a penny
In the old man's hat.
If you haven't got a penny,
A ha'penny will do;
If you haven't a ha'penny,
Then God bless you!
~ *English Rhyme*

Dimmest and Brightest Month Am I

Dimmest and brightest month am I;
My short days end, my lengthening days begin;
What matters more or less sun in the sky,
When all is sun within?
~*Christina Rosseti*

The Christmas Pudding

Into the basin put the plums,
Stirabout, stirabout, stirabout!

Next the good white flour comes,
Stirabout, stirabout, stirabout!

Sugar and peel and eggs and spice,
Stirabout, stirabout, stirabout!

Mix them and fix them and cook them twice,
Stirabout, stirabout, stirabout!
~*Traditional*

The More it Snows

The more it
SNOWS-tiddely-pom,
The more it
GOES-tiddely-pom
The more it
GOES-tiddely-pom
On
Snowing.

And nobody
KNOWS-tiddely-pom,
How cold my
TOES-tiddely-pom
How cold my
TOES-tiddely-pom
Are
Growing.
~A. A. Milne

From "Christmas Day"

Angels and Archangels
May have gathered there,
Cherubim and Seraphim
Thronged the air.

But only His Mother,
In her maiden bliss,
Worshipped the Beloved with a kiss.

Long, Long Ago

Winds through the olive trees
Softly did blow,
Round little Bethlehem
Long, long ago.

Sheep on the hillside lay
Whiter than snow;
Shepherds were watching them,
Long, long ago.

Sheep on the hillside lay
Whiter than snow;
Shepherds were watching them,
Long, long ago.

Then from the happy sky,
Angels bent low,
Singing their songs of joy,
Long, long ago.

For in a manger bed,
Cradled we know,
Christ came to Bethlehem,
Long, long ago.
~ *Anonymous*

The Friendly Beasts

Jesus, our brother, strong and good,
Was humbly born in a stable rude;
And the friendly beasts around Him stood.
Jesus, our brother, strong and good.

"I," said the sheep with curly horn,
"I gave Him my wool for His blanket warm.
"He wore my coat on Christmas morn,
"I," said the sheep with the curly horn.

"I," said the dove from rafters high.
"I cooed Him to sleep so He would not cry,
"We cooed Him to sleep, my mate and I;
"I," said the dove from rafters high.

"I," said the cow, all white and red.
"I gave Him my manger for His bed;
"I gave Him my hay to pillow His head;
"I," said the cow, all white and red.

"I," said the donkey, shaggy and brown.
"I carried His mother uphill and down;
"I carried her safely to Bethlehem town,
"I," said the donkey, shaggy and brown.

And every beast, by some good spell,
In the stable dark was glad to tell,
Of the gift he gave Emmanuel,
The gift he gave Emmanuel.
~*English Carol*

In the Bleak Midwinter

In the bleak mid-winter
Frosty wind made moan,
Earth stood hard as iron,
Water like a stone;
Snow had fallen, snow on snow,
In the bleak mid-winter
Long ago.

Our God, Heaven cannot hold Him
Nor earth sustain;
Heaven and earth shall flee away
When He comes to reign:
In the bleak mid-winter
A stable-place sufficed
The Lord God Almighty,
Jesus Christ.

Enough for Him, whom cherubim
Worship night and day,
A breastful of milk
And a mangerful of hay;
Enough for Him, whom angels
Fall down before,
The ox and ass and camel
Which adore.

Angels and archangels
May have gathered there,
Cherubim and seraphim
Thronged the air,
But only His mother
In her maiden bliss,
Worshipped the Beloved
With a kiss.

What can I give Him,
Poor as I am?
If I were a shepherd
I would bring a lamb,
If I were a Wise Man
I would do my part –
Yet what I can, I give Him,
Give my heart.
~Christina Rosseti

Merry Christmas

M for the **Music**, merry and clear;
E for the **Eve**, the crown of the year;
R for the **Romping** of bright girls and boys;
R for the **Reindeer** that bring them the toys;
Y for the **Yule** log softly aglow.

C for the **Cold** of the sky and the snow;
H for the **Hearth** where they hang up the hose;
R for the **Reel** which the old folks propose;
I for the **Icicles** seen through the pane;
S for the **Sleigh bells**, with tinkling refrain;
T for the **Tree** with gifts all abloom;
M for the **Mistletoe** hung in the room;
A for the **Anthems** we all love to hear;
S for **St. Nicholas** – Joy of the year!
~ From St. Nicholas Magazine

Jesus Ahatonhia (Jesus is Born)

'Twas in the moon of wintertime
when all the birds had fled,
That mighty Gitchi Manitou
sent angel choirs instead.
Before their light the stars grew dim
and wand'ring hunters heard the hymn
"Jesus, your King is born; Jesus is born: in excelsis gloria!"

Within a lodge of broken bark
the tender Babe was found,
A ragged robe of rabbit skin
enwrapped His beauty round.
And as the hunter braves drew nigh,
the angels song rang loud and high;
"Jesus, your King is born; Jesus is born: in excelsis gloria!"

The earliest moon of wintertime
is not so round and fair
As was the ring of glory
on the helpless Infant there.
And chiefs from far before Him
knelt with gifts of fox and beaver pelt.
"Jesus, your King is born; Jesus is born: in excelsis gloria!"

O children of the forest free,
oh sons of Manitou,
The Holy Child of earth and heaven
is born today for you.
Come kneel before the radiant Boy,
who brings you beauty, peace, and joy.
"Jesus, your King is born; Jesus is born: in excelsis gloria!"
~*Father Jean de Brebeuf*

~~~~~~~~~

At last Thou art come, Little Saviour,
And Thine angels fill midnight with song,
Thou art come, to us gentle Creator,
Whom Thy creatures have sighed for so long.

Thou hast brought with Thee plentiful pardon,
And our souls overflow with delight;
Our hearts are half broken, dear Jesus,
With the joy of this wonderful night.

~~~~~~~~~

Infant Jesus, meek and mild,
Look on me, a little child;
Pity mine and pity me,
Suffer me to come to Thee.

~~~~~~~~~

What lovely Infant can this be
That in the little crib I see?
So sweetly on the straw He lies,
It must have come from paradise.
~*Father Faber*

Christmas Eve

On Christmas Eve the bells were rung;
On Christmas Eve the Mass was sung:
The only night in all the year
Saw the stoled priest the chalice rear.

The damsel donned her kirtle sheen;
The hall was dressed with holly green;
Forth to the wood did merry-men go,
To gather in the mistletoe;

Then open'd wide the baron's hall
To vassal, tenant, serf, and all.
Power laid his rod of rule aside,
And Ceremony doffed his pride.

A Christmas gambol oft could cheer
The poor man's heart through half the year.
~*Sir Walter Scott*

~~~~~~~~~~

When Jesus called that Christmas week,
I wasn't at my best;
The house was much too cluttered to entertain a guest.
He seemed to notice everything:
the cards still unaddressed,
The gifts piled high awaiting wraps,
the baking and the rest.
His eyes fell on the evergreen and
the presents 'neath the tree.
"It's My birthday that you celebrate...

what are you giving Me?"
What am I giving Him? I thought.
Ashamed, no words I found.
So many costly things I'd bought.
He looked at me and frowned.
I prayed He'd let the question pass,
but when He did persist,
I blurted out the truth at last:
"You were not on my list."

~~~~~~~~~~

The Snow Man

One day we built a snow man;
We made him out of snow.
You should have seen how fine he was —
All white from top to toe!

We poured some water on him,
And froze him, legs and ears;
And when we went inside to bed
I said he'd last two years.

But in the night a warmer kind
Of wind began to blow,
And winter cried and ran away,
And with it ran the snow.

And in the morning when we went
To bid our friend good day,
There wasn't any snow man there —
Everything had run away!
~W. W. Ellsworth

Winter Night

Blow, wind, blow!
Drift the flying snow!
Send it twirling, whirling overhead!
There's a bedroom in a tree,
Where, snug as snug can be,
The squirrel nests in his cosy bed.

Shriek, wind, shriek!
Make the branches creak!
Battle with the boughs till break of day!
In a snow-cave warm and tight,
Through the icy winter night
The rabbit sleeps the peaceful hours away.

Call, wind, call!
In entry and in hall,
Straight from off the mountain white and wild!
Soft purrs the pussy cat,
On her little fluffy mat,
And beside her nestles close her furry child.

Scold, wind, scold!
So bitter and so bold!
Shake the windows with your tap, tap, tap!
With half-shut, dreamy eyes,
The drowsy baby lies
Cuddled closely in his mother's lap.
~*Mary F. Butts*

The Epiphany

Three kings went upon their way
To find a mightier King than they.

Three wise men, with heaven-taught eyes,
Looked for the Wisest of the wise.

The mighty ones to their Mightier
Brought gold and frankincense and myrrh.

The wise knelt to the Wisest One;
Their star had led them to the Sun.

The grown kings had their joy complete
Low at a little Child-King's feet.

All the way the kings had trod,
Seeking a King, and finding God.

Little King, greatest King,
Unto Thee our hearts we bring.
~*Emily Hickey*

Sources:

Practical Aids for Catholic Children - Sr. M. Aurelia O.S.F and Rev. F. Kirsch

Tell Us Another - Winfrid Herbst

Just Stories - Winfrid Herbst

A Child's Garden of Religion Stories - Henry P. Matimore

Anecdotes and Examples for the Catechism - Rev. Francis Spirago

Catholic National Reader Book Two

Children of the Kingdom - Beatrice Mary Fernekees

Wonder Stories of God's People - Henry P. Matimore

Legends of the Saints

Bible Stories for Children

The Ideal Catholic Readers; Fifth Reader

American Cardinal Readers

De la Salle Fifth Reader

"Good King Wenceslaus" and "Saint Thomas Becket - Archbishop of Canterbury" adapted by Brianna Zonneveld

www.ingramcontent.com/pod-product-compliance
Lightning Source LLC
Chambersburg PA
CBHW072135170626
46813CB00004BA/1580